KITCHEN THINGS

KITCHEN THINGS

AN ALBUM OF VINTAGE UTENSILS AND FARM-KITCHEN RECIPES

Richard Snodgrass

Foreword by

Christina French

Skyhorse Publishing

Skyhorse Publishing books may be purchased in bulk at special discounts
for sales promotion, corporate gifts, fund-raising, or educational purposes.
Special editions can also be created to specifications. For details, contact
the Special Sales Department, Skyhorse Publishing, 307 West 36th Street,
11th Floor, New York, NY 10018 or info@skyhorsepublishing.com.

Skyhorse® and Skyhorse Publishing® are registered trademarks of Skyhorse
Publishing, Inc.®, a Delaware corporation.

www.skyhorsepublishing.com

10 9 8 7 6 5 4 3 2 1

Library of Congress Cataloging-in-Publication Data is available on file.

ISBN: 978-1-62636-036-5

Printed in China

This is Marty's book.

In general, nothing which is intuited in space is a thing in itself, and that space is not a form which belongs as a property to things. . . . Objects are quite unknown to us in themselves . . . [they are] mere representations of our sensibility.
—*Immanuel Kant*

* * *

The moment one gives close attention to anything, even a blade of grass, it becomes a mysterious, awesome, indescribably magnificent world in itself.
—*Henry Miller*

* * *

Things do not exist without being full of people.
—*Bruno Latour*

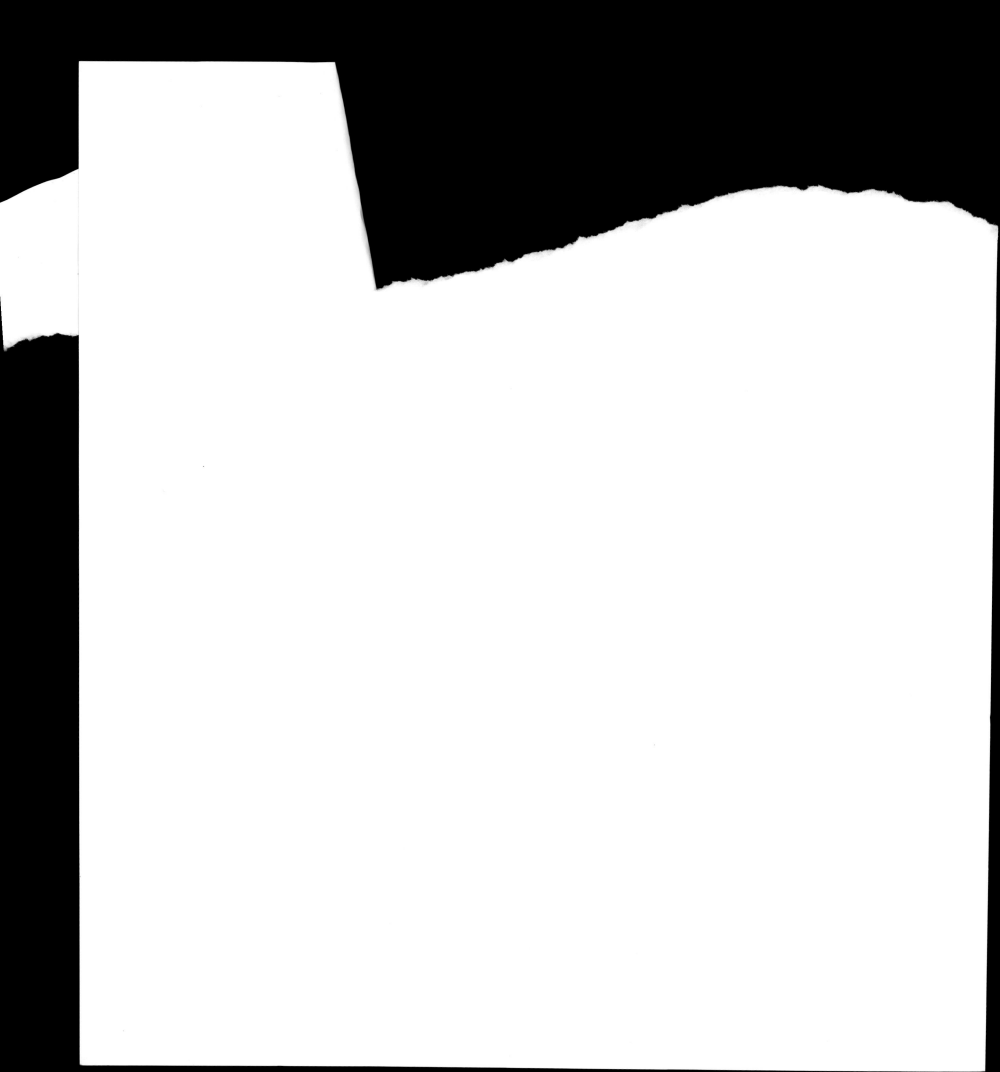

CONTENTS

FOREWORD

The eighteenth-century French epicure and gastronome Jean Anthelme Brillat-Savarin once said, "Tell me what you eat, and I will tell you what you are."

As publisher of a food magazine, I have the unique challenge of communicating this genuine power and presence of food in our lives. The challenge is rooted in the multitudes of misperceptions regarding our modern food experience: fast food, Hollywood diets, vanishing family dinners, excess and associated disease, etc. Every day, food is dissected, deformed, packaged, marketed, and consumed with more consideration and controversy than ever.

If I had to define a single purpose for *TABLE* Magazine, it would be to simplify this conversation. Slow it down. Bring food off of such a dysfunctional stage of critical performance and bring it back to our homes, our table, and our lives.

This is why the work of Richard Snodgrass has graced the pages of my publication since the first issue in 2006. Richard captures the power of this simplicity like no other artist. One simple kitchen "thing" sparks a conversation, a memory, and most importantly, a story told through the lives of his wife Marty's family members.

Richard tells stories about how a cherry pitter, dish towel, or egg cup can richly define who people are, how they live and how they lovingly (and often satirically) share the experience or history of food in their family. On their own, the images communicate an almost animal-like or unexpected human quality to the kitchen things. When paired with Richard's uncommon storytelling, the reader forms an even deeper appreciation for the true character of each thing based on the personality of the cook, the economic and cultural necessity of the times, and the influence of family tradition.

The stark simplicity of Richard's black-and-white format, the saturation of lighting, and his careful positioning of each kitchen thing, all help to bring a quieting focus to the importance of how an individual item can tell the story of people's lives.

When food and photography meet, many things can be expected—it's quite a popular topic for today's art and journalism professionals. But, in the case of Richard's work, the unexpected is delightful, as we never see the food itself. The stories of a family are told through the daily routines, specials occasions, and functional roles that a kitchen thing provides.

I like to think of Richard Snodgrass as a modern-day Brillat-Savarin, who would say, "Show me your kitchen things, and I will show you *who* you are."

Christina French
Publisher, TABLE Magazine

THE
THINGS THEY
USED

Part 1

PEPPER SHAKER

It started innocently enough. A rainy winter afternoon; I was sitting in the kitchen watching my wife, Marty, cooking chili for the week ahead—I was starved but it was to make a photograph—when I noticed this pepper shaker. Sitting with its salty companion on the counter.

Art Deco was a revolution in style that influenced the design of everything from skyscrapers to everyday items and utensils. Shakers such as this were a familiar sight during the 1940s and '50s in greasy spoons across the country. This set undoubtedly found its way to our kitchen as mementos—or relics—of a country diner called The Shantee once run by Marty's family in conjunction with their farm. But it wasn't the utensil's style, or general history, that got me interested in photographing it.

Nor did I think it had to do with the history of the spice trade, as interesting as that might be. Salt is one of the few rocks we humans ingest on a regular basis; it's critical to the survival of living things because it helps regulate the balance of fluids in the body. But earlier civilizations didn't know that level of detail, and salt was valued primarily as a preservative. That it was also a *basic taste* was value added. Pepper, on the other hand, was the king of spices, and the spice of kings. If salt was necessary, pepper was a luxury, available only to those who could afford it. These days, though, pepper seems fated to be the perpetual follower, at least in common speech. One says without thinking, "Please pass the salt and pepper." Pepper's role as the perennial runner-up is evident even in regard to this shaker's label: it may be worn thin from years of use, but the label on its companion salt shaker is completely worn away.

"What's so interesting about the pepper shaker all of a sudden?" Marty says over her shoulder as she browns ground beef in a skillet. Squinty-eyed against the heat.

"That's what I'm trying to figure out," I say. And take the shaker up to my study to make a photograph.

WOODEN SPOON

When I return the pepper shaker to the kitchen, Marty is at the sink cleaning up after her latest flurry of cooking. "That didn't do it for you?" she says. Up to her elbows in suds.

"Matter of fact, it did," I say. "But it was almost a given for a black and white photograph. Milk glass against a black background. It couldn't help but say something for itself. I'm just wondering if the same would be true for something more subtle."

For years I had photographed interiors. My intention was to portray the people who lived in a particular place, not by showing the people themselves, but by showing the objects on which they left their imprint. I thought of the images like stage settings after the players had exited, the lives themselves seen in afterimage. Now I was wondering if the same could be true for a single object.

Sticking up from the rack on the drain board, as if waving for attention, is a wooden spoon.

Now here's a utensil with a story.

Spoons of one sort or another have been around since folks in Paleolithic times realized they could use seashells to scoop up broth from a mastodon stew. When Northern Europeans began to make rather than find spoons, the utensils were of wood—the Anglo-Saxon word *spon* means splinter—that looked very much like this one. In the Middle Ages, royalty had spoons made of gold; other wealthy families had theirs made from silver, hence the saying, "Born with a silver etc., etc." In Southeast Asia, the spoon is the principal eating implement, the fork used mainly to shovel food onto the other. But credentials dating back to the prehistoric mean nothing compared to this particular spoon: it came from the kitchen of Marty's grandmother, Grandma Beard. Which makes it sacred.

Marty looks to where I am looking. "Now wait a minute."

"It's not as if photographing it will steal its soul or something," I say.

"Funny, that's exactly why I thought you photographed things."

"*Steal* seems so harsh. Let's just say I *borrow* it for a while."

My wife scratches her nose with a soapy wrist. And gives me a look that only a wife can.

WONDER SHREDDER

While Marty is busy elsewhere in the house, I take the opportunity to scout the kitchen for other utensils to photograph. The old utensils hang on the walls, gathered from her family and mine. She's used them to decorate her space, to make it her own. I decide my next subject is the Wonder Shredder—maybe as much for the name as for its potential as an image.

The setup for taking the photographs is not fancy. A white plastic egg-shaped cocoon to soften and diffuse the light—as a friend, a lighting director, says, "Soft light goes everywhere." Two light sources: to the left, a three-tube light box standing on edge; to the right, a goose-necked desk lamp with a daylight bulb. For the background, a black T-shirt, held in place with duct tape. To suspend the objects for a sense of space, a separation from the background, black string is threaded through holes drilled in the cocoon. The camera is a single-lens Rolleiflex named Rachael. (Later, I replaced the makeshift lighting and the Rollei with a digital Nikon named Josie.) As with all the utensils, before I start, I ask the Shredder if I may take its image. (To date, none has refused. . . .)

A little research shows that this Wonder Shredder is probably from the late 1920s or early '30s, and is worth about $5 these days. The "wonder" of the Shredder, I suppose, is that it's curved at the top and bottom so it can fit over the top of a bowl or angle into it, holding it in place as the shreds fall as they may. The Shredder often came in sets of three—fine, medium, and coarse—and in its day was so popular that it had a cookbook devoted to its usage. Contemporary versions are still in production, though now they come in stainless steel as well as tin. The original tin version was known for its ability to stay sharp, and its dull silvery finish is responsible for the patina that gives testament to its years of use.

That patina—the result of a surface being corrupted—is what gives this utensil its character. Its luster, ultimately its beauty. Much the same, it would seem, as it is with people.

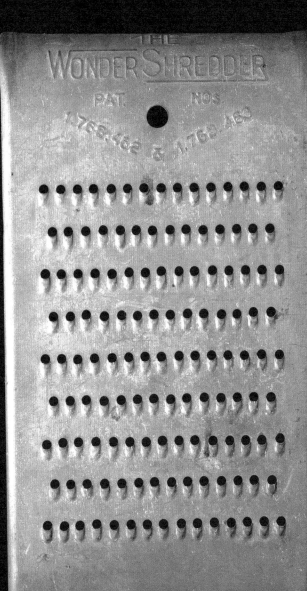

BOX GRATER

The truth is we can learn from things. They have experiences, stories to tell. The photographer Oliver Gagliani used to say a thing has a life of its own, a life-cycle just like that of a person: it has a birth, a youth when it's new and fresh and untried; then it matures to adulthood, the height of its powers and use; finally it decays and becomes broken and old.

Then there's this guy, who I nickname The Jolly Grater. (When I ask him if I may take his image, he appears to give me a grin.) The reference books and Wikipedia tell me that graters were invented by Francois Boullier in the 1540s so hard cheeses could still be used. They also say that this basic design dates back two hundred years, and who am I to argue? The advantage of this design is that it gives you as many as four graters in one; one side of this particular fellow is devoted to openings for slicing vegetables, which is why he's smiling. The disadvantages of the design are well known to anyone who has tried to clean the inside of one, where the shredding can involve fingertips and dishcloths.

The question remains, at least in my mind, why is this guy smiling? Or why do we perceive it to smile? I'm aware that one of the reasons I started to make images of these utensils—as can be said of all photography—is to see how they look as photographs. Because photography changes things; the subject is no longer the thing-in-itself, it becomes a representation of the thing. What's more, as the subject of a photograph, it becomes part of a new thing-in-itself, an image on a piece of paper or on a screen—however the photograph is displayed. The difference between art and artifact, in a way, if art is the intention. A memory of a memory as it were. Yet this jolly fellow adds a whole new element; in addition to being an image to capture the spirit of those who used it, it takes on a new or added identity as a metaphor for something else. Something other. Graters don't smile, we know that. And yet here he is, smiling. Quantum mechanics shows us that observing a phenomenon changes the phenomenon. Maybe photographing a thing not only changes the thing—it changes us.

BONING KNIFE

No collection of kitchen things would be complete without a knife or two. For that matter, the same can be said for any general collection of tools. Making tools defines the Paleolithic period, beginning around 2.5 million years ago (there were people sitting around making tools 2.5 million years ago! And today we worry about things like getting a parking place. . . .), an age that covers 99 percent of the history of basic human technology. Knives, something to cut with, were probably developed right after something to pound with. It's interesting to me that in the same time frame that people were cultivating implements to benefit themselves or do harm to others, they were also developing art as well as spiritual pursuits such as burials and rituals.

This particular kitchen knife is of the boning variety, designated as such by its sharp point and narrow blade. It probably dates from the early 1900s and comes from Marty's family farm. The stiff blade indicates it was meant for removing the bones of beef and pork—a more flexible blade is used for poultry and fish—though this fellow probably also served as a general utility knife, used for everything from cutting rope to cleaning fingernails. For a rather crude, probably inexpensive knife, this guy comes with a lot of emotional weight. Though Marty doesn't remember her father ever using it, Marty's mother—the Legendary Chub—called it Bill's Knife, referencing it to her late husband, when she loaned it to me to include in this series. Family lore claims the knife has its narrow blade from being honed so much, but that, unfortunately, is only the stuff of legend.

Still, looking at the handle, worn smooth over the years from the grip of calloused hands, the blade mottled from being cleaned of blood and offal, there remains something of the spirit of the men and women who have used this knife. Images of a barnyard on an early winter's day, fog drifting in the distant fields, steam rising from a scalding vat, the carcass of a hog hanging from a block and tackle . . . images of a camp deep in the woods, figures around a fire, dogs resting under the black trees, the sound of a knife on a whetstone as someone recounts stories of hunts in the past.

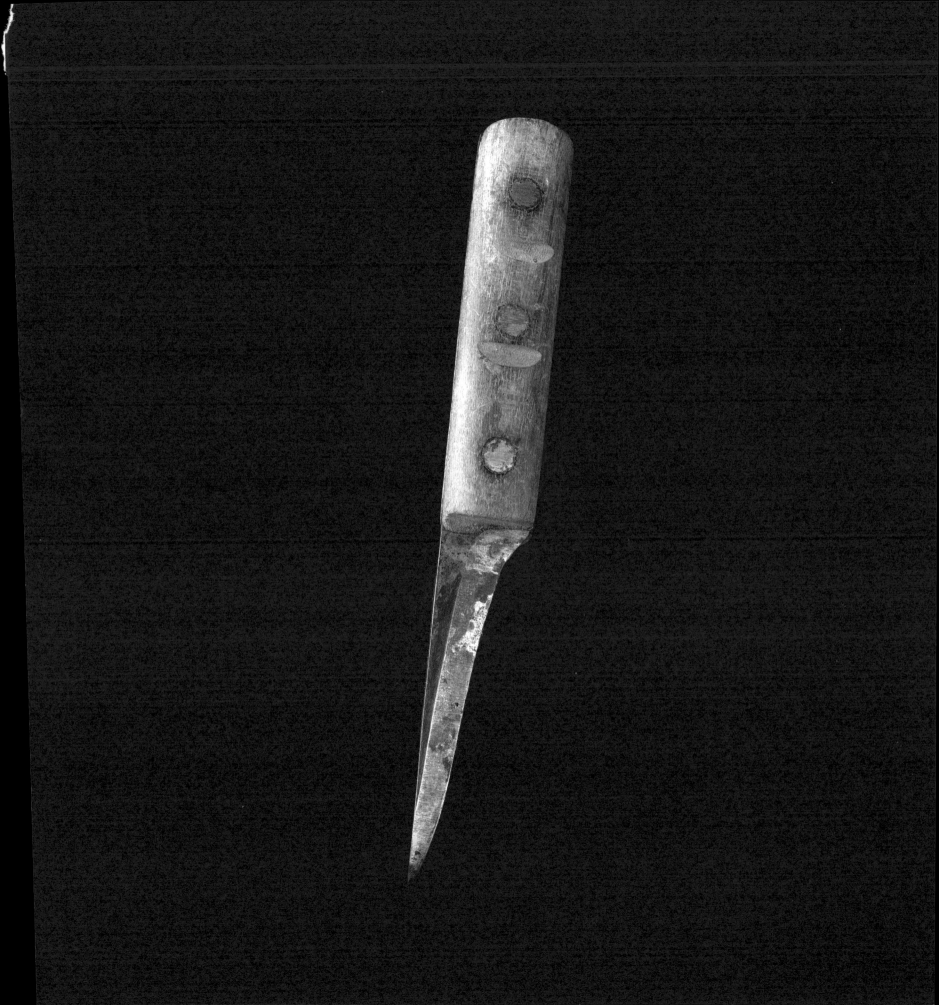

POTATO MASHER

And this: hanging on the wall above the sink (How many times did I look at it and never see it? Or see it and never look at it?): a potato (or vegetable) masher (also called a beetle, though beetles are generally wooden pestle-like implements), circa 1900, not from Marty's family farm this time, but from the other side of the family, the sainted Grandma Beard. (I am fortunate, for the purposes of this series of kitchen things, that I have a wife who is fond of decorating with antiques; I am likewise fortunate that we both come from families who rarely threw anything away.)

One source defines a masher as "an instrument for beating vegetable pieces to a pulp," the idea of which—beating something to a pulp—may be the origin of the popular threat. This type of masher, with a metal head consisting of crisscross or zigzag wires or a thin plate with holes or slits, derives from the mashers made from a single piece of wood that were used in the Victorian era. In 1847, a gentleman by the name of Lee Copeman patented the design because of "his love of smooth, lump-free mashed potatoes." Another source considers the genre of mashers and pestles to be the oldest kitchen utensils in use today, though I would question such a claim—what about knives and spoons? Be that as it may, these utensils have a long history, and not only for mashing vegetables: in *Mrs. Lincoln's Boston Cookbook* of 1884, a potato masher is used to press finely-chopped meat into cloth bags for sausages.

Other common uses include mashing apples for applesauce; pumpkins and rutabagas for soup; beans for refried beans; chickpeas for hummus—or just about any soft food you can think of that needs a good mashing. Of course, cleaning all those little wires before the era of the automatic dishwasher is a different matter. It's easy for me to imagine such a handy kitchen utensil transformed into a magic wand for spreading bacteria.

"That sounds like you," Marty says, reading over my shoulder. And I wonder—as only a husband can— *What did she mean by that?*

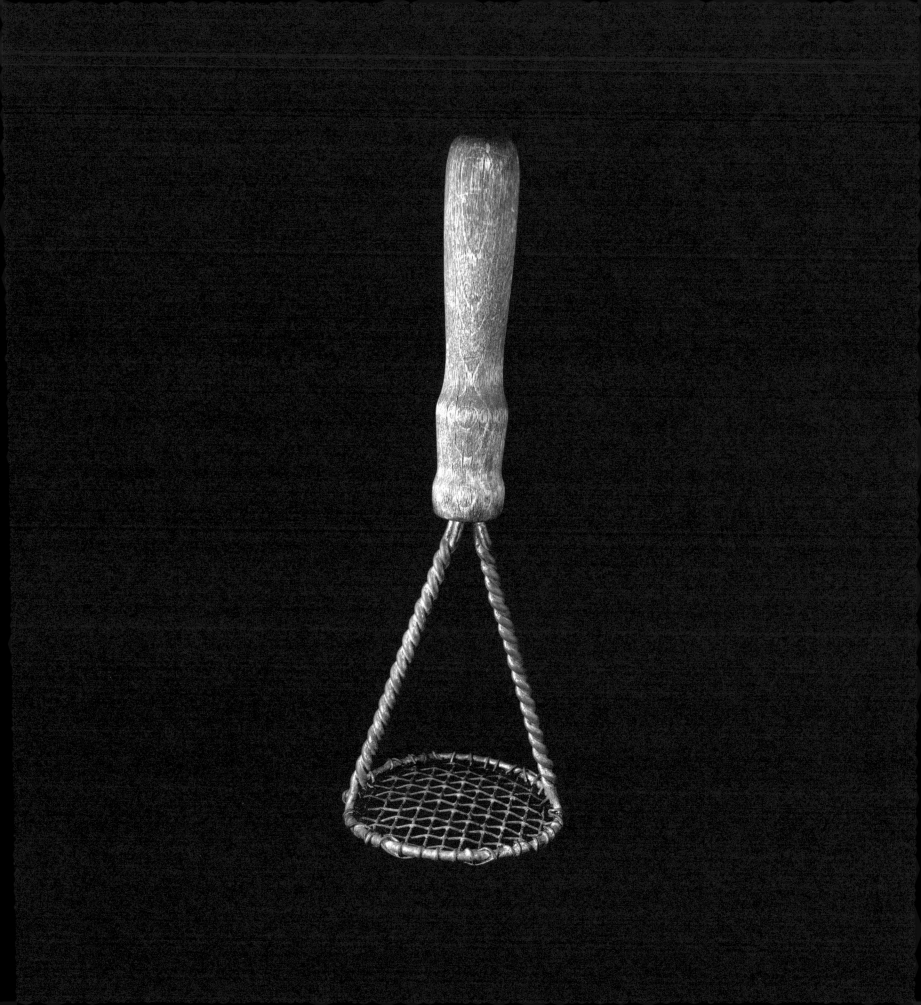

MASHER

"I get it. It looks like a foot," Marty says when I show her the image on the screen.

"It's another masher. Like the one you got from Grandma Beard's."

"And don't forget to put Grandma Beard's back on the wall where you got it."

"Of course I won't forget," I say and give her a look into the side of her face that says *Sheesh!*

Having indeed forgotten to return it.

"Where did you get this one?"

"I don't think it's from my family. I must have picked it up at a flea market somewhere."

"Is that why you photographed it? Because it looks like a foot?"

"I didn't realize it until I saw it on the groundglass. I just thought it was interesting. I heard it calling to me, 'Dick, Dick! Over here by this stack of bowls . . . !'

She leans nearer the screen. "A four-toed masher. Is that anything like a three-toed sloth?"

"Depends on who's doing the mashing. Some are more slothful than others. On the other hand—or foot, as it were—if you turn it around, it's a five-toed masher."

"I don't think I'd want to mash my potatoes with something that looks like a foot."

"They stomp grapes with feet to make wine, don't they?"

"That's different," Marty says, shaking her head. "The alcohol would kill the germs."

"You know that's not true, don't you?"

"Of course. But I'm going with it anyway. But with this, you'd have mashed potatoes squeezing up between the toes."

"Like toe-jam."

"Yuck! Double yuck! No thanks. I'll stick to Grandma Beard's."

"You would anyway. Because it was Grandma Beard's."

"And don't forget to put it back where you got it."

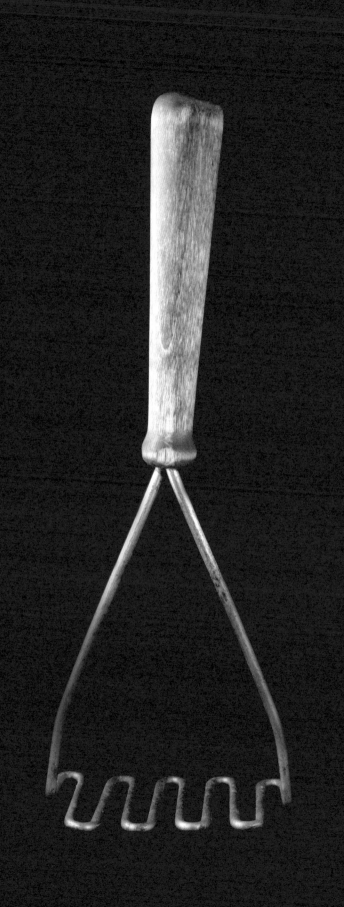

BEETLE

This is a true, unmistakable beetle, a potato masher of the Old Order. Linked invariably in Irish cooking, to a dish called champ, also known variously as poundies, cally, bruisy, and—my favorite—thump. The dish combines boiled potatoes (beaten to a pulp) with warm milk, butter, and scallions. The importance of the beetle in all of this is shown in a traditional poem:

There was an old woman
That lived in a lamp.
She had no room
To beetle her champ.

She's up'd with her beetle
And broke the lamp,
And now she has room
To beetle her champ.

The potatoes were usually beetled in large quantities, a strenuous exercise at best, with the iron pot held in place by a hole in the cottage floor. Hence, the term *pothole*. The dish is served in a large mound with a well of butter in the center. There are detailed instructions that it should be eaten only from the edges, working your way in, dipping each bite in the butter. But any kid knows that.

When I included this photo in a recent show, I was surprised that some folks found this photograph not only sexually suggestive, but also, in one instance, the image of a dildo. Fascinating. Well, for each of us, the world is as we see it. I do confess that in addition to the beauty of the utensil in itself, the process of photographing it called to mind other associations. In addition to the spirit of the people in my family who may have used it to beetle their champ, I think the lines are reminiscent of a slender-waisted woman in a hoop skirt, with a very long and graceful neck.

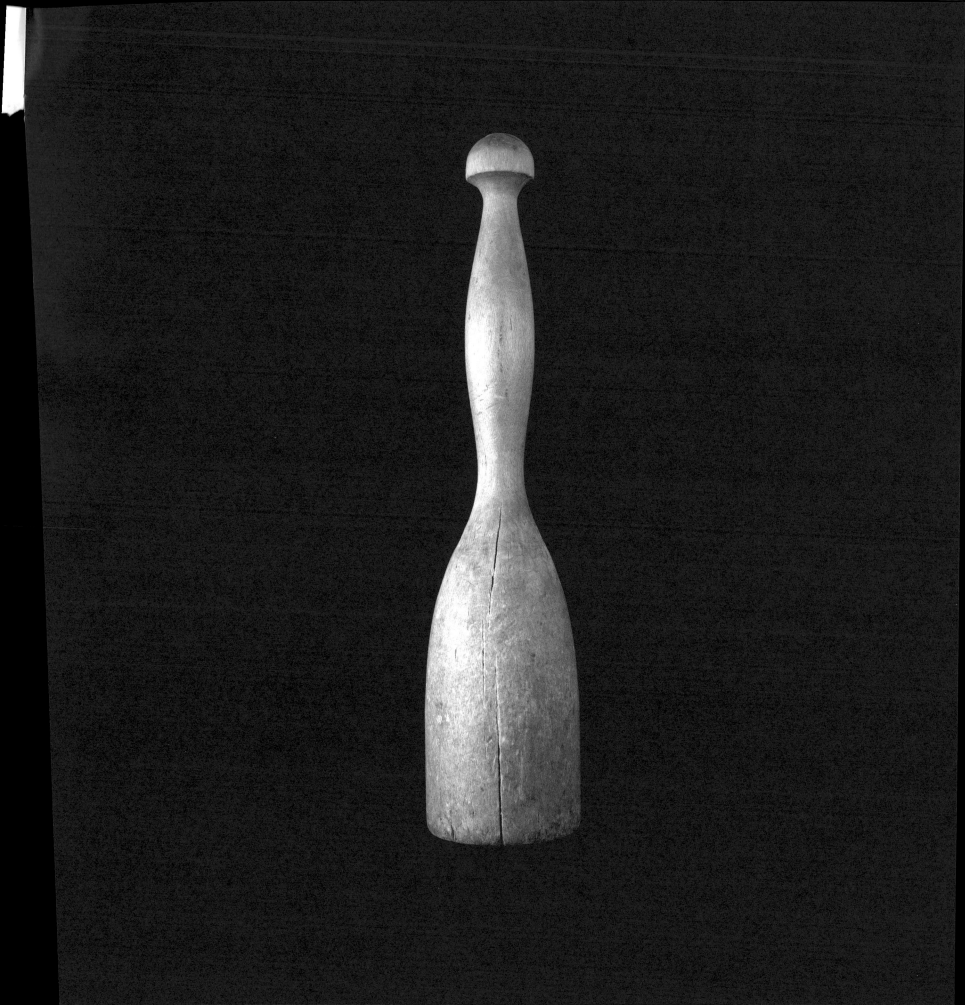

ALL-PURPOSE OPENER

Metaphor is the essence of art (with a capital "A"). Art has to do with levels of meaning, and metaphor is the express elevator to take us to those levels or layers of meaning. Without levels of meaning, a work is in the realm of craft, or reportage, or representation or the like—all good things, of course. Qualities that can be appreciated and enjoyed for their own sake. But Art gives something more. Art, depending upon its intention and skill and efficacy, can include all these qualities, and then add emotional content, insights, wisdom as well. And metaphor is the means through which we reach those depths. Or heights.

Take this all-purpose opener. The photograph is, if I do say so myself, a pretty good representation of the thing-itself. If you were sent in search of an all-purpose opener, you could use this image to tell you what such an animal looks like. And I think the image gives a sense that this guy has a history, a story to tell, he's done its share of work in his day, passed through his share of working hands. A survivor from the age of neighborhood Five & Dimes and local hardware stores.

And yet, and yet . . .

In the process of becoming the image of a photograph—part of a new thing-itself—it has taken on added dimensions. Looked at in a certain way, this fellow is rather scary. A made-up monster from a Grade-B sci-fi thriller from the 1950s perhaps. Or a nightmare figure from a Hieronymus Bosch view of the Underworld. The horrific, gaping mouth of a Goya painting, or a study of the human condition by Francis Bacon. Vertical Picasso-esque eyes. Key-adorned headdress or helmet or *tablita*. Corkscrew penis. Small pointy tail. Fear and associations being in the eye of the beholder, the same as beauty. The point being that now this utensil can be seen as something else, something more than a tool for opening cans and bottles. And yet, it's that, too. Something to ponder over. Conjure with.

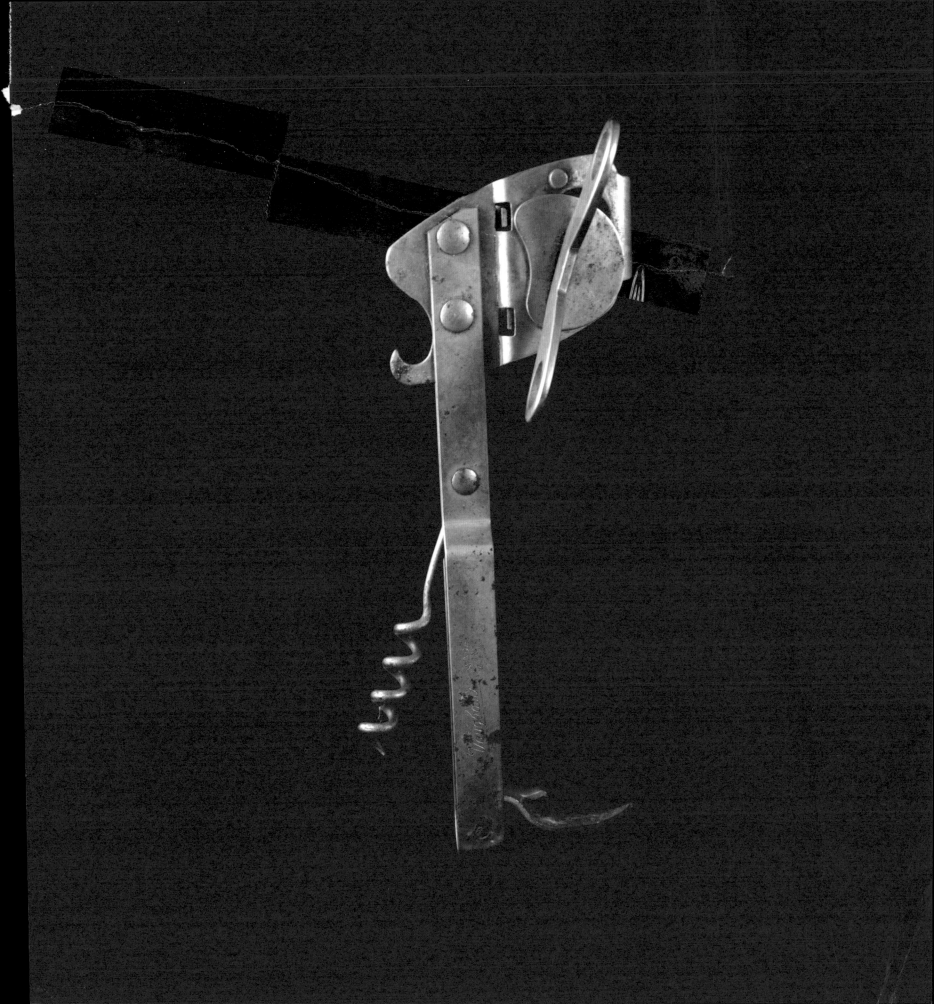

CAN OPENER

Likewise, this opener looks too much like an angry dude to be comfortable. The guy in the car behind you who thinks you cut him off. Whatever is bothering him, he needs to get over it and get on with his life. A can opener he was born, a can opener he shall always be.

The history of the can opener (or tin opener) is contingent upon, as you might expect, the history of the can. Though who first came up with the process of canning—preserving food in airtight tin cans—seems a matter of some dispute. The Dutch Navy is said to have used such a process as early as 1772. Then again, Napoleon is often credited with helping develop the practice with his offer of a prize to whoever could come up with a way to preserve food for his far-flung *Grande Armée*. The winner of the prize in 1810, a confectioner named Nicolas Appert, was successful in preserving food by sterilization, though his process used glass bottles. In the same year, an Englishman, Peter Durand, received a patent from King George III for a similar process using tin-plated iron canisters—hence the name *can* and the verb *to can*. (Why the name *canning* stuck for the homegrown effort of preserving food in mason jars is another of life's little mysteries.)

The first commercial canning factory opened in England in 1813, and the containers were soon in use by the English Navy. But there were problems. For one thing, the best skilled craftsmen could only make six cans a day. For another, the container was essentially a large iron pot that weighed more than the food inside. By 1846, the thickness of the metal slimmed down, and tin canning was more widely adopted through a method that could produce sixty cans a day. But there was still the issue of the solder. The tins were sealed with poisonous lead solder that, if it came in contact with the food, could have deadly results. The most famous example was the Artic expedition conducted by Sir John Franklin in 1845, where crew members suffered extreme lead poisoning after eating canned food for three years. That particular wrinkle didn't get worked out until the invention of the steel can and the introduction of the side seamer in manufacture.

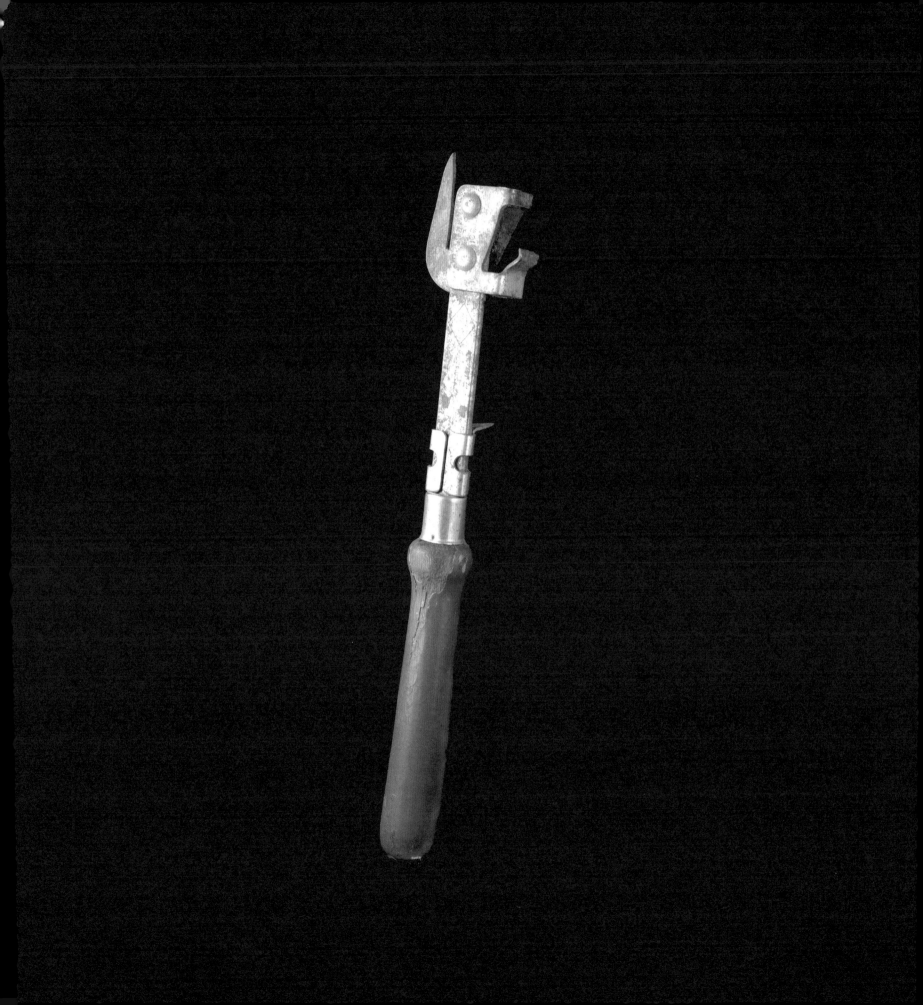

CAN OPENER

When friends and acquaintances learn that I'm working on a series of kitchen things, they begin to send me their own finds from looking around their kitchens, from their own forays to flea markets and secondhand shops. Which is iffy. I find I can't photograph just any object that comes my way; not to sound precious, but the utensil has to speak to me in some way. There needs to be some indescribable, indefinable quality that interests me enough to go through the process of making a photograph. Which again is iffy. People, I find, tend to be very protective—if not downright defensive—about their kitchen utensils. "What! My can opener is much more interesting than *that* can opener!" Still, I decide to work with this guy, sent to me by a friend because . . . well, he not only said hello, but he also seems to be directing traffic.

Actually, this opener is very close in its basic design to many of the very first openers, which started to be manufactured in the mid-1800s. Before that, you were pretty much on your own. Early entrepreneurs were good at developing methods for putting food in containers, not so good at getting it out. The first cans carried the instruction: "Cut round the top near the outer edge with a chisel and hammer." It was only with the development of thinner steel cans that openers could be devised.

The first opener, patented by Ezra Warner of Waterbury, Connecticut, in 1858, resembled a bent bayonet. But it was specialized equipment for its day and not to be trusted to just anyone; the opener stayed at the grocer's, and lids were removed before the cans were carried home. In 1865, an opener for home use was included with cans of pickled beef named Bully Beef; in an early example of coordinated marketing, the head of the cast-iron opener looked like a bull. (A later version of the opener looked like a fish, but I see no mention of Fishy Beef).

Can opening was further democratized with the invention of the cutting wheel opener by William Lyman in 1870, and the Star Can Company of San Francisco introduced the serrated rotating wheel in 1925. The electric can opener arrived in 1931, but there are folks who refuse to believe there's a legitimate need for such a thing.

ROTARY CAN OPENER

"It looks like a semaphore," Marty says.

"It's an early geared can opener. At least I think that's what it is."

"Or a guy sending signals with those semaphore flags. I tried to learn that once when I was in the Girl Scouts."

"There's only one arm."

"Then maybe he's sending only half the message, like shorthand. Would that make it short-arm? Why'd you say you *think* that's what it is?"

"Because I can't find any mention or example of it in the reference books. I figure it must have been a design that didn't catch on and didn't stay around very long."

"Or a design that didn't work very well."

"Or that too. Which would be why it didn't stay around very long."

"That's sad to think about. Once upon a time there was a whole bunch of people involved with making it, a factory somewhere where it was made. Somebody's dream of success. Of making a killing. And it all disappeared because the thing didn't work the way it was supposed to."

"A common problem with dreams," I say.

"Maybe that's what the one-armed semaphore guy is signaling." Marty stands up and begins jerking her arm in different positions over her head, down to her side, across her body. "P-l-e-a-s-e f-o-r-g-i-v-e m-e-I-d-o-n-t w-o-r-k v-e-r-y w-e-l-l."

"Don't forget I photographed it mainly because it's an interesting-looking can opener."

"A can opener that's interesting-looking because it looks like a semaphore guy."

With that, Marty waves her imaginary flag in figure-eights in the air as if celebrating something and parades back to the kitchen.

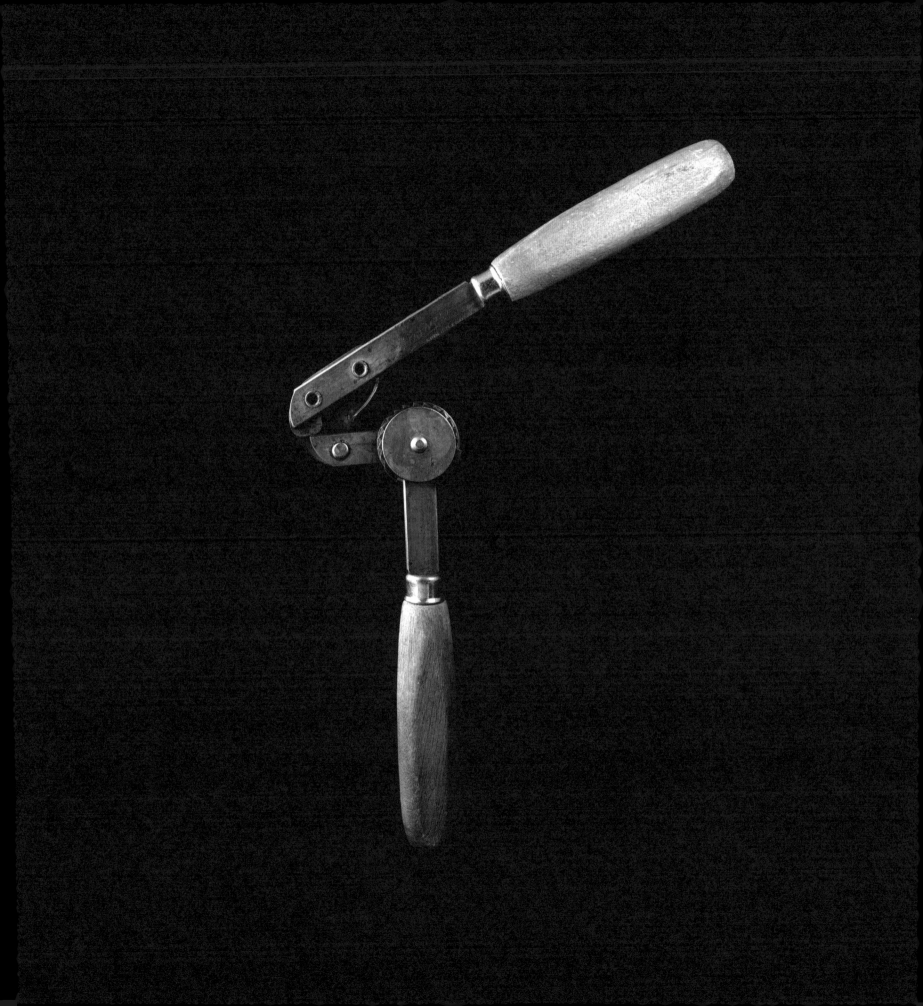

CORN SHUCKS

Aw shucks!

This promised to be a very straightforward discussion regarding these two little guys (each is only three to four inches long) called *corn shucks*. But things are seldom as simple as they first seem. The question here is the difference—if there is a difference—between corn *shucking* and corn *husking*.

About corn, however, there is no discussion. Unless, of course, you call it *maize*, as they do in technical journals and the British Isles and in Spain and a large part of the rest of the world. Corn is a grain, often misclassified as a vegetable, derived from a grass that was domesticated by the Indians of Central America as early as 12,000 BC. Eventually its cultivation spread throughout the Americas, and European explorers in the fifteenth and sixteenth centuries carried it throughout the world. Today corn is the most widely grown crop in the Americas, though most of it is used as feedstock.

These two utensils from the early 1900s demonstrate a homemade answer to an age-old problem with corn—actually one of two problems, depending on what you think these guys are for: either separating the cob from the husks, or separating the kernels from the cob. On one hand, the reference books I consult all say that corn *shucking* involves removing the husks and the silk from the cob. On the other hand, the elderly woman in the antique store in the Ohio Corn Belt who sold them to me, as well as a number of farmers I asked, said that shucking is the process of removing the kernels from the cob. I ask Marty's mom, the Legendary Chub, who was born on a farm and taught school to farmer's children. She gives me her best schoolmarm's head-tilt. "I would say, if you're removing husks, it's called *husking*. Where did you get these old corn shucks?"

My research, however, turns up Little Miss Cornshucks. Mildred Cummings was an African American who did a cute "rural maid" routine to get gigs in nightclubs in the 1930s and '40s, but whose "serious" singing, including her career song, "So Long," blew folks away, influencing singers such as Ruth Brown and LaVern Baker. She was another who wasn't as simple as she first seemed.

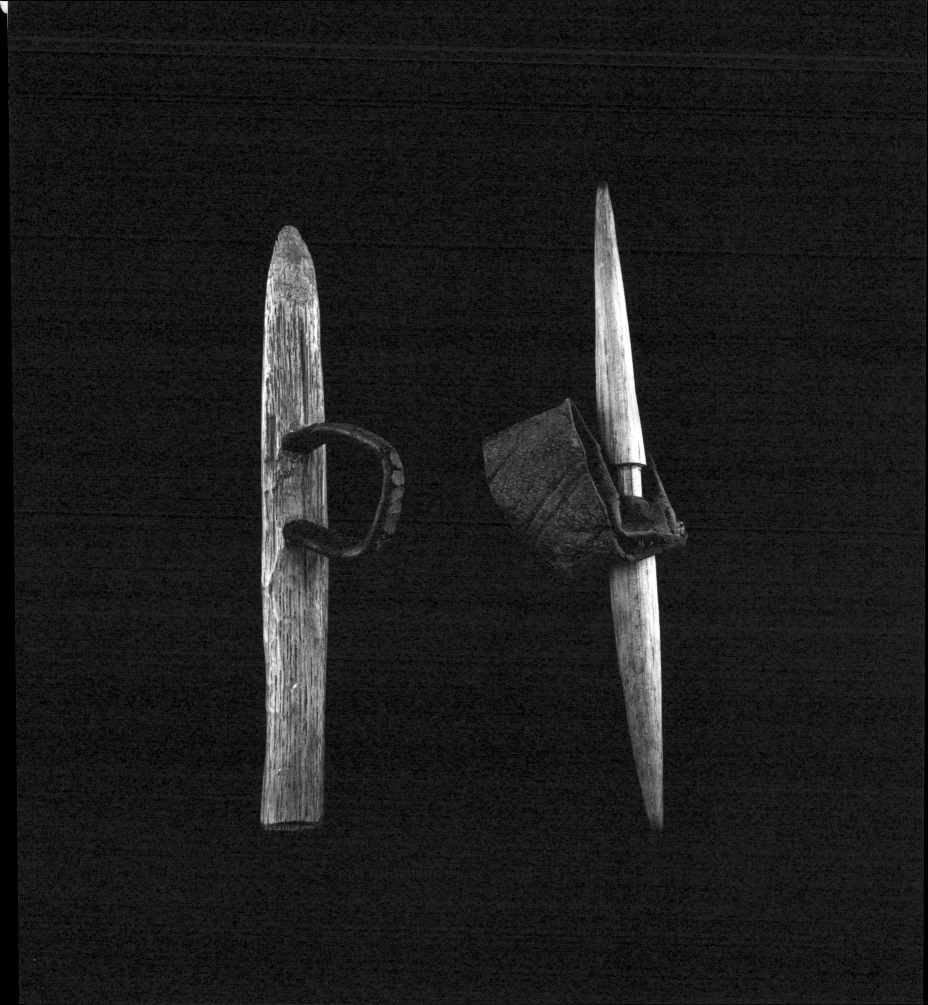

PEELER

For many of us, the vegetable peeler was our introduction into the grown-up world of kitchen utensils and food preparation. Wanting to help in the kitchen, we certainly weren't allowed to handle a finger-slicing implement such as a paring knife, nor could we be trusted with electrical appliances such as a mix-master or blender. But given a vegetable peeler, a child could scrape away at a pile of potatoes or carrots and feel that he or she made a contribution to the meal.

This particular vegetable peeler is of the Yorkshire or Lancaster variety, invented by a nineteenth-century blacksmith named Thomas Williams who lived, one assumes, in Yorkshire or Lancaster. The other common variety of peeler resembles a safety razor, the blade perpendicular to the handle, variously known as a Y-peeler, Rex Peeler, Yoke Peeler, or Speed Peeler. In addition to its twin in-turned blades, the Yorkshire Peeler features a shaft that swivels on its axis, the better to follow the contours of the vegetable. Some people find this annoying and wish it would just hold still. There is also a distinctive rattle to the swivel, a jolly little jingling that evokes memories of peeling sessions past. The nub of the shaft facilitates the displaced violence of gouging out the eyes of a hapless potato.

The peeler pictured here is from the early 1950s and is remembered fondly by the Legendary Chub as one of the first kitchen utensils she purchased when she got married. In addition to evoking a sculpture by Henry Moore or a one-legged Martian dancing on pointe, it bears an uncanny likeness to certain fertility fetishes from prehistoric cultures. Perhaps some future archeologist from a space colony will return to abandoned Earth, dig up one of these peelers, and make odd assumptions about what our culture valued in regard to procreation.

The standing debate with this type of peeler is whether you drag the implement toward you (while rotating the vegetable in the opposite direction) or whittle it from you. For myself, I find I usually start out with every intention to create a continuous spiral peel that will amaze family and friends, only to end up hacking away in a mad fury as the slivers fly.

ICE CREAM SCOOP

Frozen desserts made with milk or cream were known to the ancient Chinese, Greeks, and Romans, and ice cream as we know it was popular throughout the Middle East by the tenth century. Recipes on how "to *ice cream*" appeared in England and America in the eighteenth century, and confectioners sold *iced cream* during colonial times. But it took modern refrigeration to make ice cream more than a treat for only special occasions.

The utensil pictured here is a true ice cream scoop, as opposed to an ice cream disher as the first lever-action dispensers were called. In the 1930s, Sherman Kelly of Toledo invented what's claimed to be the world's best ice cream scoop. All metal, with a handle filled with heat-conductive fluid, the Zeroll was designed to roll the ice cream into a perfect ball. (Zero-roll, get it?) But the intention wasn't aesthetics. By not squeezing the ice cream, the dispenser could get more servings per gallon.

Our scoop here is of the consumer variety, but with the same gaping mouth as the professional models, reminiscent of a hungry baby bird or perhaps Edvard Munch's *The Scream*. (The idea that Munch's painting portrays an ice cream headache is just silly.) It looks simple enough, but a lot of factors are at work to get a proper somersault of ice cream. There's the coefficient of friction, with the flow against the metal scoop, to say nothing of the coefficient of thermal expansion as the size of the metal changes with the change of temperature. The laws of thermodynamics are involved somewhere—none of which I pretend to understand—as well as gravity, fulcrums, speed of acceleration, kinetic energy . . . the mind reels.

But the greatest mystery to me is how ice cream, coldest of treats, became a comfort food. A solace for the lonely heart. Why, when that special someone doesn't call, we find ourselves sitting in a corner of the sofa, tablespoon in hand, keeping company with a tub of Butter Pecan. Why, when love plays hide-and-seek, we search the evening streets, holding a cone before us like a supplicant's candle, moving through the uncaring crowds with our two scoops of Jamoca Almond Fudge.

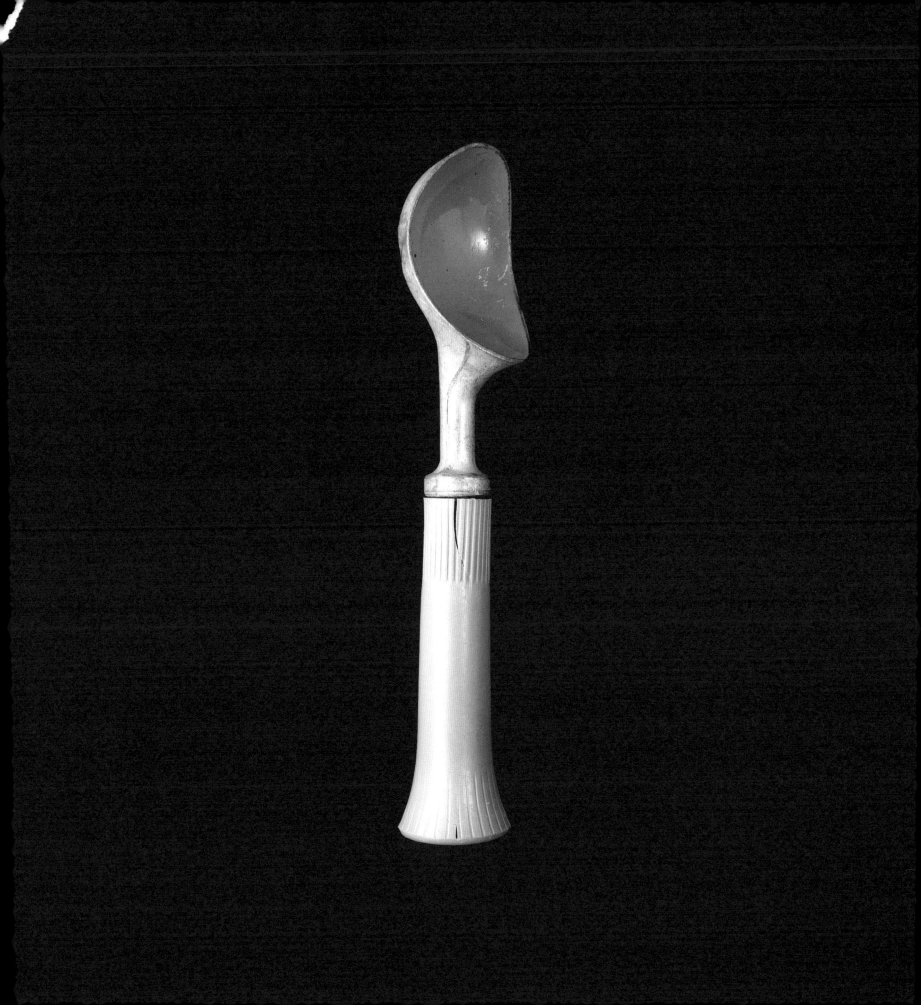

SQUEEZER

Misunderstanding makes the world go 'round. The result in most cases, I suspect, from differences of perception. Take this toothy fellow, for example. A coworker from my wife's office contributed it to this series, saying it was her garlic press. However, when I included it in an exhibition of my work, a woman informed me—in no uncertain terms, I might add—that it was a lemon slice squeezer. "Don't be ridiculous," said her friend, "it's an ice cube crusher." At this point, I have no idea what it is.

No wars or divorces resulted from the above differences, though I can see how such misunderstandings can escalate. Added to that are the problems with perception itself. In his book *The User Illusion*, Tor Nørretranders demonstrates how, of the estimated millions of bits of information that sweep through our senses at any given moment, only a tiny fraction reaches our awareness. The rest is simply discarded because we can't process it all. What's more, it seems our consciousness is on an inherent time delay. There is approximately a half-second interval between the sensation of a pinprick and our conscious awareness of it. And in that half second, our bodies can do miraculous things on their own or interject all sorts of preconceived baggage. We think that we experience the world directly and that the self is the initiator of actions, but such is not the case. Our world is a simulation, a description of reality if you will, and we struggle to catch up with what we already know.

All that and we haven't even touched upon how the imagination gets involved. As I made this print, I was reminded of a Peter Max–like creature, something that might swim in an octopus's garden with a yellow submarine. But as Mark, the owner of Sewickley Gallery who handles my work, hung it for a show, he told me, "I love the seagull." My wife's friend, however, probably had the last word when she heard about these divergent opinions: "I don't know a thing about all that," she said. "I just want to know when you'll be done with my garlic press."

BALLER

One of the enduring mysteries of photography is how this purely mechanical (and chemical; and, now, digital) medium can convey the intentions and emotions of the person making (or taking) the photograph. It's one thing to ascribe such qualities to the hand-wrought lines of a painting or drawing, the caress of hands on a spinning potter's wheel, even the taps of a hammer on a block of marble. It's another matter to ascribe them to the result of holding a box full of mechanisms and clicking a button. But I've seen too many examples of a photographer's unbridled emotions coming through an image to doubt it.

This kitchen thing is another whose purpose seems to be up for grabs. It's obviously to create some kind of ball, but speculations as to the food involved so far have included melon, meat, and ice cream. The truth is that its purpose isn't why I made the image. I photograph some of these objects because they carry the mark and aura of the people who have used them. Some are interesting for the beauty of their lines and forms. For others, I'm simply curious to see how they would look as photographs. But from the get-go (curious phrase, that) with this fellow, I was interested in it as a metaphor.

A metaphor works with emotional associations below our conscious level, unlike a symbol, say, which is more concerned with concepts or abstractions. In regard to these kitchen things, sometimes my initial contact is merely a whisper through my inner thoughts that says there is something here worth investigating. As I studied this particular object on the camera's groundglass, my whimsy initially got the better of me and I thought of Doctor Doolittle's Pushmi-Pullyu. But I soon realized that what this utensil made me think of were two people having a conversation. I can't tell you what was particularly on my mind the day I made this image, but I do know that whenever I see it, I take heart that these two halves are part of a whole that, with the proper application, can come together as one.

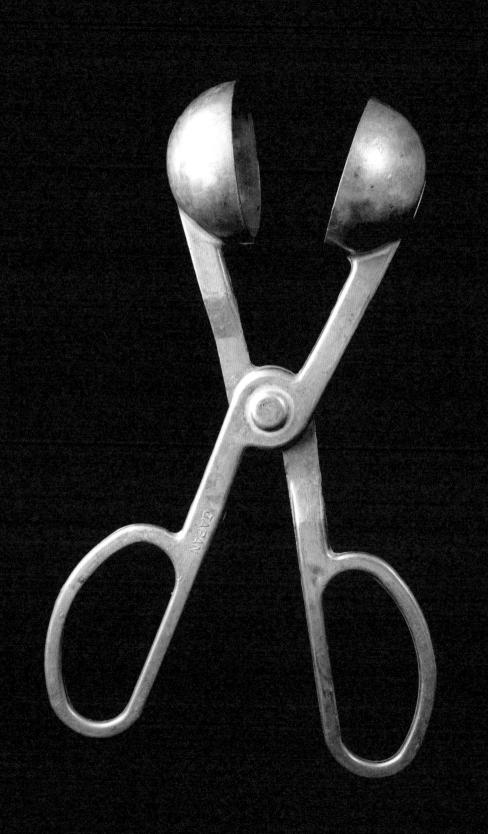

RICE STRAINER

This rice strainer—complete with a leftover grain of rice—was sent to me by the photographer Linda Connor, who got it on one of her trips to India. In the world of metaphors, I'm tempted to focus on the potential sexual nature of the image—the bumps at the top of the handle could be from a prehistoric fertility doll; and, of course, there's that gaping strainer at the base—but the more mundane food story here is equally interesting. In the words of the classic *Saturday Night Live* skit, "Sometimes a banana is just a banana, Anna."

That solitary grain reminds us that rice is a major food staple for two-thirds of the world's population, providing more than one-fifth of its daily calories. There may be more corn (maize) grow around the world, but much of it is used for things other than human consumption. Because rice can grown almost anywhere and is well-suited to countries with high rainfall and low labor costs, it is critical for maintaining populations worldwide, often those of Third World or developing countries, especially in East and South Asia, the Middle East, Latin America, and the West Indies. In the United States, folks who eat rice tend to have a healthier diet in general, including more dietary fiber, meat, vegetables, and grains. The thing is, when most Americans eat rice, they do so by choice, the result of education or ethnicity/race, rather than in the rest of the world, where it's a matter of survival.

This rice strainer reminds me of something else. All these kitchen things, if you think about it, whether handmade or mass produced, are basically copies of some original made centuries ago; the designs may change through the ages, but there was a time when an early man or woman first decided to form a web of fibers or leaves in the crook of a stick to make the first strainer, an instant when many different someones in many different places and times discovered that it was easier to cut off a piece of flesh from a mastodon or gazelle with a sharp-edged flint rather than tear it with his or her teeth. Things not only have their individual life spans; they have their own timeline through history, interwoven with—though totally separate from—ours. There is a civilization of things.

MEXICAN WHISK

"A drum major's baton."

"It's a Mexican whisk."

"To whip up a meringue?" Marty puts one hand on her tummy, holds the other above her head, and does a few rumba steps.

"You're thinking of merengué. Meringues are said to have originated in Switzerland with a pastry cooked named Gasparini."

Marty gives me a look that says, *You missed the funny part.* "Or a wizard's magic wand. *Shazum!* You're a soufflé!"

"It's another thing Linda sent me. To quote, she said 'It deserves to be photographed.'"

"Why would she say that?"

"I guess because it's rather unique. You have to admit it's not your everyday whisk."

"With good reason. I wouldn't think it would beat an egg white worth a darn."

"True. And whipping it around a bowl would undoubtedly bend the blades."

"To say nothing of the health factor. If you think the beetle would turn into a germ wand, imagine what's growing inside that thing. A portable breeding ground for Montezuma's revenge."

"Maybe it was meant to be a decorative item."

Marty, whose decorative tastes run to the practical and historical, personal or otherwise, looks at me as if to say, *Not on my kitchen wall you don't, Buster.*

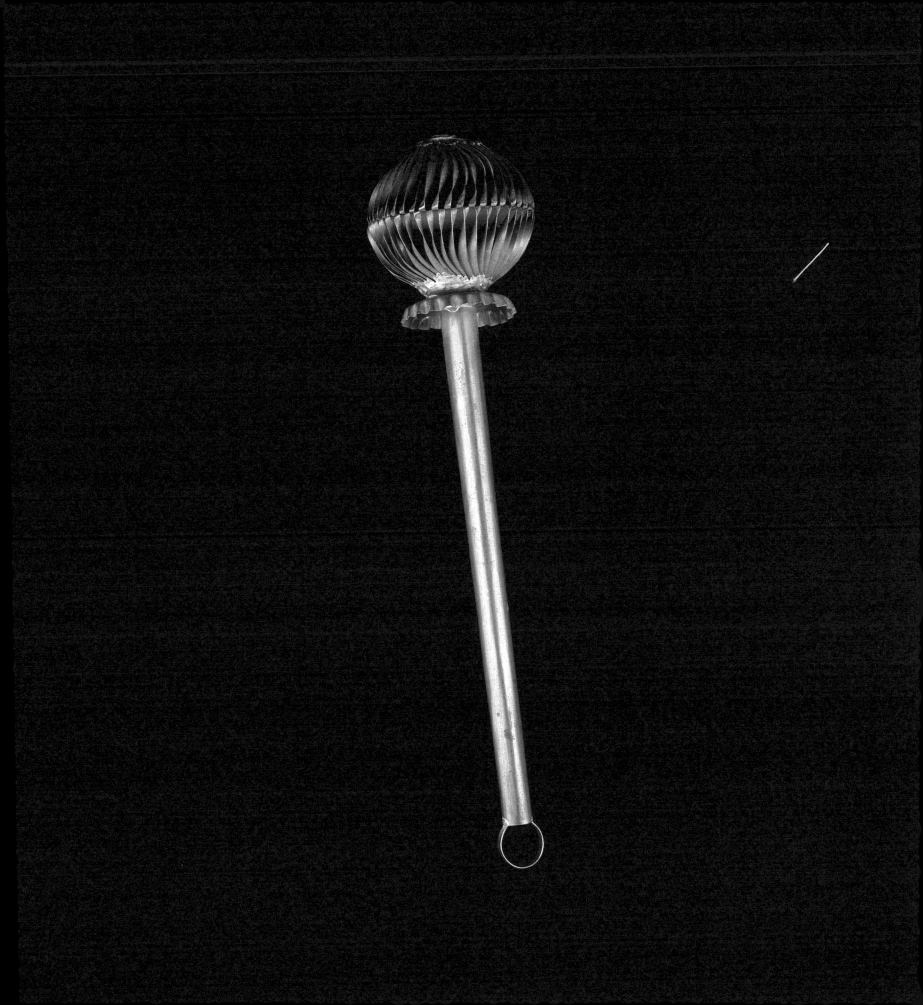

SPIRAL WHISK

Blame it on Julia Child. In the process of popularizing French cooking, Child's PBS show in the 1960s and '70s canonized the humble whisk. Suddenly bouquets of whisks and wooden spoons blossomed on the countertops of young marrieds and Julia devotees. The whisk became a badge of honor that declared "A Gourmet Cook Lives Here." At one time in an earlier marriage, my wife and I prepared so many soufflés that I was afraid my right forearm might swell up like Popeye's. It was a relief—and unwittingly prescient—when we no longer measured our success as a couple on the perfect puff, rising like a chef's toque above the rim of the pleated bowl.

This particular whisk—they are also called whips, as well as whisk whips and sometimes even whip whisks—is of the bedspring coil or churn beater variety. It is happiest with light liquids in small bowls and is used with an up-and-down motion, much like a pogo stick or a very active bedspring (don't go there). I'm not sure how it is thought of now, but back in the day, this type of whisk was considered more of a gadget, something found in a variety or hardware store, not Williams-Sonoma. Oh the shame!

What's interesting to me is the spiral at the end. Found in every prehistoric culture, such symbols were dismissed during the heyday of Modernism as futile attempts by unenlightened people to deal with life's terrors and ecstasies. But these symbols keep popping up in unexpected places, like burps from our collective dreamlife. In our age, the spiral is a handy if flawed two-dimensional representation of a non-linear, four- (or more) dimensional reality—part of the infamous space–time continuum—a concept familiar, interestingly enough, to both modern physics and Hopi Indians. With its ever-expanding, ever-contracting whorls of space and time, the idea of the cosmic spiral offers the spooky possibility of at some point meeting oneself coming back the opposite direction. If I do have such an encounter, I hope to learn, among life's other mysteries, if anyone along the way has discovered an easier method to whip a soufflé into proper shape.

FLOUR SIFTER

Bang the drum slowly.

Even when you use this guy for what he was intended—sifting flour—one is tempted to use it as a percussion instrument. A metal maraca. A barrel tambourine. A distraction to the serious baker as memories of kindergarten rhythm bands come sprinkling down.

Flour is probably as basic a food as you're going to find, at least among those food groups that aren't walking, flying, or swimming about. Wheat flour is particularly important to Western, Middle Eastern, and African countries, and corn (or maize) flour continues to be a staple in Latin American cooking. But these are only two of many "flours." You can make flour from just about any kind of plant stuff, if you care to; a casual search came up with more than sixty different kinds, my favorites being Old Man Saltbush Flour, Wry Wattle Flour, and Witchety Bush Flour, all from Australia, mate.

Here in the United States, we're most familiar with wheat flour, though anyone who has studied the labels of bread and crackers will tell you that the designation *wheat flour* is not always what it at first seems. The word *flour* itself comes from *flower*, which comes from the Old French *fleur*. An on-going problem with wheat flour has always been preservation; as soon as the fatty acids of the germ of the wheat plant are exposed to air, it begins to turn nasty. An early solution during the Industrial Revolution was to simply separate the germ from the rest of the plant, which increased the shelf-life considerably. Unfortunately, without the germ, the resulting flour lacked vitamins and all those healthy amino acids. Well, it probably seemed like a good idea at the time.

Flour is the common denominator of those things we call "baked goods"—breads and cakes, pastries and pies, cookies and crackers—though it's also in pasta and used as a roux to thicken sauces and gravies and in coating for fried meat, fish, and vegetables. I personally find it thought-provoking that white wheat flour is also the traditional base of wallpaper paste.

FOLEY SIFTER

The clever sifter pictured here replaces the traditional side-crank with a squeeze mechanism so you can accomplish the operation with one hand. Thus building up your grip as you sift away.

Nowadays, flour is often labeled Pre-Sifted, but woe betide the baker who falls for that. True, one of the original purposes of sifting was to remove impurities and foreign matter, such as pieces of the grist stones that might have broken off in the process of milling the grain. Modern manufacturing methods and steel rollers have pretty much solved those problems. But there is still the matter of settling. Flour left to its own devices will compact in a sack or container, the flour on the bottom weighing as much as 25 percent more than the flour higher up. Supposedly, with today's processed flours, instead of sifting you can use a technique fetchingly called scoop-and-level, also known as dip-and-sweep. (Why am I reminded of the phrase "crash-and-burn"?) The idea is to stir your scoop or cup in the container to aerate the flour, then get a heaping measure and level it off with the back of knife or other flat surface. Good luck with that. Others prefer to simply weigh the ingredient and be done with it.

Which brings up the issue of measurement. It turns out that there's a world of difference between the recipe that calls for "one cup of sifted flour" and "one cup of flour, sifted." In the case of the former, it means to sift the flour before or while you measure; the latter, to sift the flour after you measure. It's that density thing again. Confusing the two can result in a cake with the taste of cardboard (or wallpaper paste), or one fit for a flagstone. Your guess is as good as mine when a recipe calls for "partially sifted flour."

Another benefit of sifting is that it can blend the dry ingredients of a recipe before adding any liquid. That can result in the flour being sifted twice: once in the initial measure, and again in the blending. If you started with pre-sifted flour, the result could be a cake so light it might threaten to float off the plate. Of course, a good sour cream icing would help weigh it down. I'm just saying....

PASTRY BLENDER

A pastry blender, also called a pie crust mixer or flaker, is used to mix—known in this context as cutting in, not to be confused with taking someone else's partner on a dance floor—hard or solid fat (such as butter, shortening, or lard) into flour to make pastries. The description alone is enough to add several pounds to the waistline.

Pastries are dough made of flour, fat, salt, and water rolled out and used to cover or envelope sweet or savory fillings. They're distinguished from bread because of their higher fat content, which creates their flakey or crumbly texture. The basic types of pastries are: Flaky (self-explanatory); Shortcrust (crumbly rather than flaky); Puff (you guessed it); Choux (think éclairs, or open-ended hors d'oeuvres filled with cheese or tuna); Phyllo or Filo (strudels; baklava); Hot Water Crust (meat pies); Suetcrust (you don't want to know); and Sweet Dough (made with yeast and lots of sugar; think: cinnamon buns, Danish, you get the idea). The essential difference between these types is how the fat is introduced into the recipe.

Which is where our pastry blender comes in. Fancy pastries—the ones we think of eating with the little finger extended—are temperamental things; they don't like to be handled too much in the making. They also like their ingredients to be kept cold, which raises obvious problems when you're working with fat. A traditional way of working the fat into the flour is with two table knives, like scissors, one in each hand. A kinder, gentler method is with a blender—even though it looks like an exotic kind of brass knuckles—which "cuts in" the fat before the flour has time to protest.

A pastry, you might say, is like a lover. It needs to be handled delicately in the making. Rich, enticing, something to look forward to—but best taken only on occasion and in small measures. Over indulge and you can feel bloated, what was once a treat now cloying, making you even sick at your stomach. Notice I said lover. Not a loved one. Or a beloved. That's more in the category of your daily bread. The staff of life. An Irish soda bread, perhaps, with no currants or raisins.

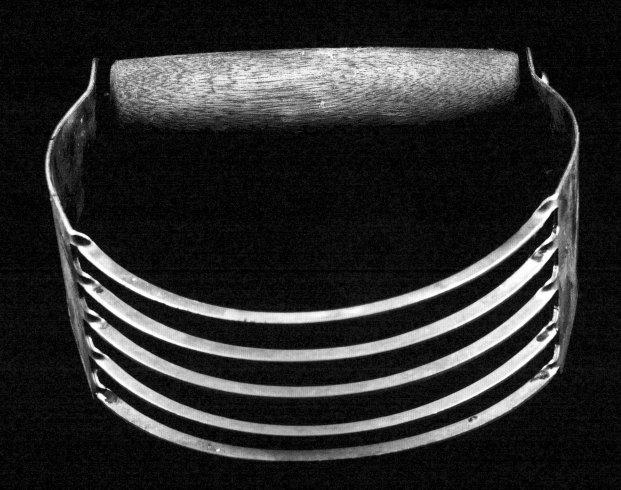

GLASS MEASURING CUP

"So now you're giving advice on love? I thought this was a book about kitchen things."

"It is about kitchen things."

"So, to quote Tina Turner, 'what's love got to do with it, got to do with it?'" Marty, arms extended above her head, raises the roof as she works her hips a couple of times.

"It was only an analogy."

"It seemed pretty particular on the subject of lovers."

"Remember, I did have a life before I met you. . . ." *Alarm! Torpedoes! Dive, Dive!* "But of course, in the most important aspects, I had no life at all until I met you."

Marty's look says, *Nice footwork, Mr. Astaire.* "And you likened me to a soda bread?"

"You know I love soda bread. I make it all the time—"

"Another analogy?"

"At least I didn't call you Dumpling."

"And why would you?"

"No reason at all."

"I wouldn't think so."

"Definitely not." *Whew!* "Okay, maybe I did get a little carried away about love and lovers."

"Speaking of carried away. Where are you taking Grandma Beard's measuring cup?"

"I'll be careful with it. I know it's sacred."

"It's not 'sacred,' silly. It's just that it was Grandma Beard's."

I think but don't say: *That's what I said: It's sacred.* I only make it to the doorway.

"Not even with currants or raisins?"

"You know I love you just the way you are." I toast her with Grandma Beard's measuring cup and head back to my study.

MEASURING SPOONS

If it weren't for Fannie Farmer, our recipes might still call for a lump of butter or a palmful of flour. Ms. Farmer was an early proponent of Domestic Science, a movement in education whose later manifestation gave us the high school home economic classes that taught me why I'll never be a baker. In her cookbook, first published in 1896, Fannie insisted that "[a] cupful is measured level . . . a tablespoon is measured level." Fannie taught generations of homemakers the basics—she's consulted regularly in this household to be sure—and established the units of measure we use today. Little wonder she is still known as The Mother of Level Measurements. *All hail!*

In the United States, a standard set of measuring spoons includes ¼ teaspoon, ½ teaspoon, 1 teaspoon, and 1 tablespoon. One might assume that 2 teaspoons equal 1 tablespoon, but it's actually 3. As for the basic question, is a regular teaspoon or tablespoon equal in size to a measuring spoon, the short answer is yes. The fact is the terms *teaspoon* and *tablespoon* are unofficial measurements; one set of spoons can vary from another as much as 25 percent. If you're truly dedicated, you can find sets of spoons with exact measurements for such inexact quantities as the Tad, the Dash, the Pinch, and the Smidgen. For a Dollop or Splash, I'm afraid you're on your own.

Spoon is also a term used for heavy-duty cuddling, a couple lying front to back, or back to front as the case may be, depending on whether one is referring to the Cuddler or to the Cuddlee. In a recent *New York Times* opinion piece, a writer talked about how his wife often calls out in the middle of the night, "Spoon! Spoon!" meaning that she wishes to be held in such a manner. The writer noted that out of love for his wife—and probably for the peace and harmony of his marriage—he always complies with her request. Although other utensils can similarly nest, it's easy to see how a wife's motives could be grossly misinterpreted if, in such a situation, she were to call out, "Fork! Fork!" As for the set of measuring spoons in this image, one can envision a veritable orgy of cuddling behind closed drawers.

MEASURING CUPS

Picture of a family of four awaiting an arrival:

"Is it coming yet?"

"I can't see anything."

"Mom, Quarter keeps stepping on my rim."

"Quarter, leave your sister alone."

"Everybody hold still and keep an eye out."

Measuring cups and spoons have been around since at least 1826, but they weren't found in most households until much later and required instructions on how to use them. In doing research for this book, I found that instructions on how to use these fundamental utensils are apparently still necessary for a lot of folks, though I have to admit that some of the directives seem painfully basic:

- There is no substitute for measuring ingredients accurately.
- It's always easier to scoop a heaping tablespoon than it is to scoop a level one.
- Fill the measuring cup to the appropriate line, place it on a level surface, and read it with your eye at the level of the liquid.
- You're best to do any measuring away from the bowl in which you're mixing things—that way, if an *Oops!* occurs, it won't ruin what you already have in the bowl.
- Measure a liquid in a measuring spoon by filling it full.
- Don't put a wet or oily spoon into a canister of a dry ingredient. You will only make a mess.

A testament, I suppose, to what's obvious to one person can be a revelation to another.

ROLLING PIN

"Nothing says baking like a rolling pin," I say. "Too bad we don't have one."

"Hold your horses," Marty says. I am then presented with the south-end-of-Marty-headed-north as she gets down on hands and knees and begins rooting through the cabinet under the dry sink. In a moment, arm inverted, she waggles a rolling pin over her back.

"Ah, another sacred relic of Grandma Beard," I say.

"Nope. Great Aunt Mary E," she says, back on her feet. "Other side of the family."

I knew of Great Aunt Mary E (as opposed to Great Aunt Mary D) as the spinster on Marty's grandparents' farm. G.A.M.E. came to her brother's farm after she bit her other sister-in-law on the ankle. There she took over the cooking chores. Whether anyone wanted her to or not.

Rolling pins come in two general varieties. Rods are basically wooden pins like broom sticks, some thick, some thin, often referred to as the French or Asian style. Rollers, such as the one pictured here, have a revolving barrel that encase the shaft, theoretically making rolling the dough easier. In addition to being the traditional weapon in popular culture of the angry housewife, they are also handy for running over one's thighs for poor circulation—but I'm not dispensing medical advice.

Great Aunt Mary E's specialty was icebox butterscotch cookies. I say to Marty that the cookies must be a treasured holiday memory. "Not really," she replies. "They were always rock hard, even soaking them in milk didn't phase them, and her recipe was for seventeen dozen so we had to eat them forever. My teeth hurt just thinking about them."

"Didn't anyone ever tell her not to make so many?"

"Are you kidding?" Marty says. "You'd never say a thing like that to Great Aunt Mary E. She wouldn't even allow anyone near the kitchen when she was cooking."

The woman was tiny, but formidable. Family legend has it that when Great Aunt Mary E was in full flight, everyone kept their ankles covered.

CHRISTMAS COOKIE CUTTERS

Cookie cutters have quite a storied past. Their ancestors were the molds for cookie pictures used in Egypt and elsewhere as early as 2500 BC. Greek slaves taught baking to the Romans, who shaped dough for religion and royalty. At the same time, Germanic tribes pressed out picture cakes during the Winter Solstice to offer as sacrificial gifts to Wotan. In the Middle Ages, gingerbread bakers either carved their own molds or worked with skilled woodcarvers to develop designs with symbolic meanings. Eating the right kind of picture cookie was thought to produce qualities such as courage, good luck, or sexual prowess. Booths with picture cakes were a main attraction at fairs and festivals. Deeply religious themes existed side-by-side with good-natured erotic imagery. Later on, picture cookies became picture messages announcing births and weddings and the like.

Eventually, the molds became all metal and moved from the hands of bakers to those of homemakers. In our country, the story goes that itinerant tinsmiths would create cookie cutters from scrap left over from roof jobs and other projects and give them as presents to the families who hired them. The first manufactured cookie cutters were produced after the Civil War when industries tried to find substitutes for a war economy. By the 1920s, aluminum became the preferred material for the cutters. Though the set pictured here from the late 1940s reflects Christmas–Christian imagery, a friend tells me that in the same period you could find sets for Hanukkah. In today's all-absorbing multinational America, I would expect to find cutters for Hindus, Muslims, Buddhists—or anyone who wants to add whimsy to baking cookies.

Sad to say, the term *cookie cutter* has come into disrepute, meaning something that lacks originality, that is the same over and over. Anyone who has ever used one of these devilish implements knows it's not that easy. Reindeer missing legs; bunnies without ears; headless snowmen—one learns to make do without body parts. As for the supposed joy of digesting a gingerbread man extremity-by-extremity, I always found it overrated and somewhat disconcerting.

PIE TRIMMER

"Sing a song of sixpence . . . four and twenty blackbirds baked in a pie." Matter of fact, during the Renaissance, when great banquets were the rage, live blackbirds were indeed baked into pies, as well as rabbits, frogs, turtles, and other small animals—even dwarfs—all to be released when the crust was cut. In the 1900s, the architect Stanford White embellished the tradition for a banquet he arranged for Diamond Jim Brady: a naked girl popped out of an enormous pie, walked the length of the banquet table, and jumped into Diamond Jim's lap. Talk about having a lot of crust.

Obviously, the crust in these pies was not of the light and flaky kind. Pies known as gallettes originated in the Stone Age when early Egyptians wrapped shells of ground wheat, rye, and/or barley around honey and baked them over coals. Later the Greeks developed pie pastry by wrapping a flour-water paste around meat to help seal in the juices. But until recent times, pie crusts were mainly inedible, or only consumed by those with strong teeth and an equal hunger. Early pies with crust coverings were called coffyns or coffins (meaning a basket or box, though the word carried the funeral sense in England as early as 1520); open-crust pies, more like our casseroles, were called traps. In both cases, the crust was the baking container itself, often several inches thick, which also served as the serving dish and storage container. Round, shallow pie pans were known in England at the time of the Pilgrims, and American pioneer women used them to make pies to stretch ingredients, literally "cutting corners." Early settlers spreading westward developed endless regional adaptations of the dish and often ate pie in some variation—either as the main course, a side dish, or dessert—with every meal. Which may help explain why pie-baking contests remain a staple of county fairs.

The utensil pictured here, officially known as a Vaughn's Pie Trimmer & Sealer from the 1920s or '30s, is variously classified as a jagger, crimper, pie wheel, pie iron, cutter, and—my favorite—giggling iron. In my research material, it bears the unhappy epithet as the "cheapest of all," but the worn handle tells me that over the years this fellow helped satisfy many an appetite.

CAKE SERVER

"Let them eat cake," as Marie-Antoinette famously said during a time of famine, the epitome of the callousness of the Haves toward the Have-Nots, helping to make the lady, Madame Deficit as she was known, a reviled figure down through the ages. Except Marie-Antoinette wasn't the one who said it. . . . Who actually did, though, is up for grabs. It was probably Marie-Thérèse, the wife of Louis XIV, one hundred years before Marie-Antoinette was born. Fact is, Marie-Antoinette was a generous patron of charity and quite concerned about the plight of the poor, though it sometimes had to be pointed out to her. What's more, there were no severe famines during the reign of her husband, Louis XVI. There wasn't even cake as we know it; the statement refers to brioche, a luxury bread enriched with eggs and butter.

You could write a book about the history of cake, and many people have. One problem with relating the history of cake is that it's hard to define exactly which ingredients to include. Cakes date back more than two thousand years, the one common ingredient being flour, which is why cakes and breads are often interchangeable through the ages. The precursors of modern cakes—round with icing—were first baked in Europe in the mid-1600s, though it wasn't until the 1800s that cakes as we know them, made with extra refined white flour and baking powder instead of yeast, came about. Cakes are thought to be traditionally round because ancient breads and cakes were made by hand and naturally relaxed into rounded shapes; the ancients also used them in religious ceremonies and their rounded shapes symbolized the sun and moon and the cyclical nature of life. Early Americans considered cake a symbol of well-being, and we continue to serve cakes at holiday, birthdays, weddings, funerals, and baptisms. In other words, if it's a significant event, let them eat cake.

In keeping with that social convention, this particular cake server, picked up at a flea market, bears the legend on its handle, "McDonough Funeral Parlor, Beallsville, PA." A marketing effort to keep the facility's name close at hand (as it were) as the mourners attended an after-funeral dinner. Though I guess calling it an instrument of death would be facetious even for me.

THE
THINGS THEY
ATE

Part 1

AUNT LIBBY'S RECIPE BOX

"These are basically farm recipes," the Legendary Chub tells me as we sit down at her dining room table to go through her recipe boxes. I ask her what it means to be a "farm recipe." "Back when these recipes were collected, in the '30s and '40s and '50s and even the '60s, farm wives didn't usually have a car at their disposal, so they couldn't simply go to the market any time they needed something. They had to have a larder well-stocked with the basics and essentials, and then make do with what they had on hand, what was either growing in the garden or put up in jars. There's nothing here that you would call fancy. Or if there is, it's farm fancy—and that's no fancy at all."

The first recipe box we tackle is Aunt Libby's—that's her in the photograph of the open box, peeking up over her recipes, though why she kept a picture of herself as a young woman in her recipe box is a mystery. Libby was Chub's aunt, Marty's great-aunt, a sister of Chub's father. Libby was raised a farm girl but became a teacher for a couple years in Indiana, Pennsylvania—among her students was a young Jimmy Stewart. She lost her position in the Depression when the School Board wanted only teachers who came from the area, and she moved to Pittsburgh, becoming in time the Postmistress at the Carnegie Mellon University Post Office. She settled in the Friendship district of town, a predominantly Italian–Polish area, keeping close to her roots by living near the Fourth Presbyterian Church, a tiny congregation that eventually joined the more theologically conservative Evangelical Presbyterian Church. Her partner was her cousin, Jessie— Chub heads me off at the pass with a stern look and says, "Don't even think it. They were only friends"— who was a social worker.

Most Friday nights, the two women drove down to Hickory and spent the weekend at Uncle Clare and Aunt Helen's—Clare, another brother—where Libby often cooked. Libby and Jessie were favorites of all the kids of Marty's generation, introducing city culture in the form of books and games—Jessie was known for getting down on the floor to play. Most of the recipes in Libby's box are ones she collected during her visits to the farm and took back to Pittsburgh. Libby and Jessie may have worked in the city, but their hearts—and their taste buds—were back at the farm.

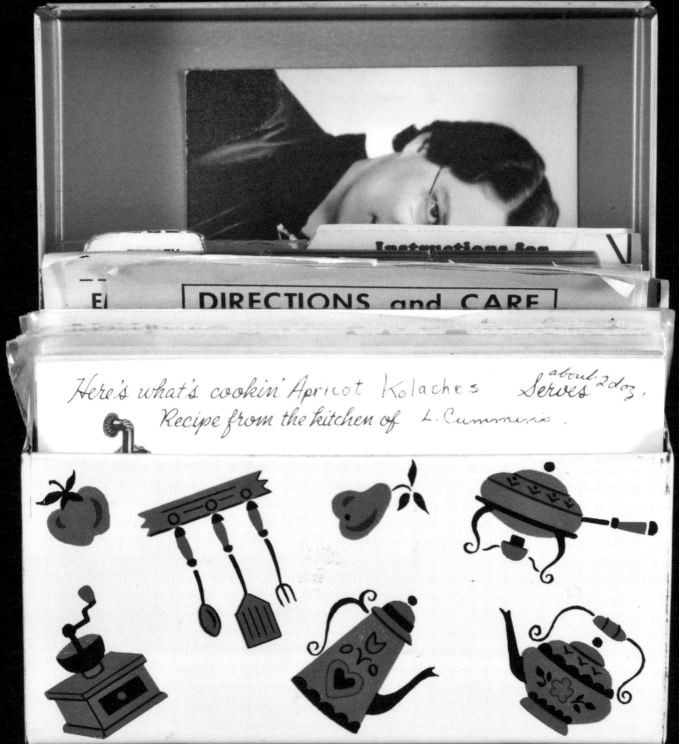

Here's what's cookin' Apricot Kolaches   Serves about 2 doz.
Recipe from the kitchen of L. Cummins.

Instructions for

DIRECTIONS and CARE

PORK CHOPS IN SOUR CREAM

"It says sour *dairy* cream," I say.

"That's easy," Chub says. "You just add a tablespoon of vinegar to a cup of cream and there you are—you're sour."

"So that's different than what you get in a little tub?"

Chub gives me a look that says, *this city-boy son-in-law is going to make for a long afternoon.*

Ingredients
6 Porkloin chop cut ½" thick
¾ t dried sage, crushed
2 T shortening (optional)
2 medium onion, sliced (1 cup)
1 t instant beef bouillon granules
½ c. hot water
½ c. sour dairy cream
1 T all-purpose flour
2 T snipped parsley

Method
Trim excess fat from chops. Set aside.

Put chops with sage, sprinkle with salt and pepper. Heat shortening or trimmings. Brown chops, drain. Add onions. Dissolve bouillon granules in water. Pour over chops. Cover, simmer 35 to 40 min., or until tender. Transfer meat to platter. Keep warm. Skim excess fat from drippings. Measure ½ c. drippings and set aside.

Combine sour cream and flour. Slowly stir in reserved drippings. Return all to skillet. Cook and stir until bubbly. Pour over meat, garnish with parsley. Makes 6 servings.

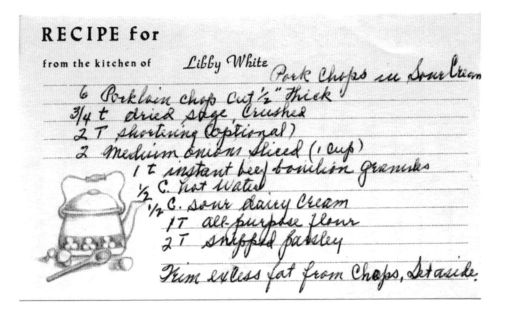

RECIPE for

from the kitchen of   *Libby White*   Pork Chops in Sour Cream

6   Porklain chops cut ½" thick
3/4 t   dried sage, crushed
2 T   shortening (optional)
2   medium onions sliced (1 cup)
1 t   instant beef bouillon granules
½ C. hot water
½ C. sour dairy cream
1 T   all-purpose flour
2 T   snipped parsley

Trim excess fat from chops, set aside.

Put chops with sage, sprinkle with salt & pepper. Heat shortening or trimmings. Brown chops, drain. Add onions. Dissolve bouillon granules in water. Pour over chops. Cover, simmer 35 to 40 min, or until tender. Transfer meat to platter, keep warm. Skim excess fat from drippings. Measure ½ C drippings & set aside.

Combine sour cream & flour slowly stir in reserved drippings. Return all to skillet. Cook & stir until bubbly. Pour over meat, garnish with parsley. Makes 6 servings

MEAT SCOFFLE

"Meat Scoffle sounds awful," I say, trying for a joke.

"Actually, this sounds pretty good," Chub says reading it over.

"What's a scoffle?" I ask.

"I haven't the foggiest," she says. "When you eat something in a hurry, you say you *scoffle* it down. Or some people say that," she adds, implying that polite people don't scoffle. She continues reading. "This sounds like a kind of soufflé for leftovers. Maybe that's what whoever wrote this meant and couldn't spell." She looks at me and bats her eyes.

Ingredients and Method

Melt 2 tbsps. butter in a frying pan, add 1 cup milk, season with salt and pepper. Stir until froths. Add 1 cup of any good leftover meat (ground fine). Simmer a few minutes, then stir in the beaten yolks of 2 eggs. Cook a moment longer. Cool, then stir in the beaten whites of eggs, put in buttered baking dish and bake 20 minutes. Enjoy!

MEAT SCUFFLE

MELT 2 tbsps. butter in A frying PAN, Add 1 cup milk, season with SALT & PEPPER. Stir until it Froths. Add 1 cup of Any good LEFTOVER MEAT (ground fine). SIMMER A FEW minutes, then stir in the BEATEN yolks of 2 Eggs. Cook A moment longer. Cool, then stir in the BEATEN whites of Eggs, put in buttERED baking dish And bAKE 20 minutes. Enjoy!

PORCUPINES

"These are fun," Chub says. "It's your ground beef and you mix it up with all the other ingredients, and you include some uncooked rice in there. Then you shape the mixture into balls, and when you cook them the rice sticks out like quills. They're great for kids. You'd probably like them too."

Ingredients
¾ lb. ground beef
1 T. minced onion
2 t. baking powder
½ c. milk
½ t. pepper
1 t. salt
⅓ c. **uncooked** rice
1 can tomato soup
1 t. dry mustard

Method
Combine all ingredients except soup. Form into 8 balls. Place in small roaster or casserole. Pour soup over balls and bake uncovered 35 minutes at 400°. Cover. Bake 35 minutes longer.

Here's what's cookin': __Porcupines__　　　　　　　　Serves: ___

Recipe from the kitchen of: _____

3/4 lb. ground beef
1 T. minced onion
2 t. baking powder
1/2 c. milk
1/2 t. pepper
1 t. salt
1/3 c. uncooked rice
1 can tomato soup
1 t. dry mustard

(over)

Combine all ingredients except soup

Form into 8 balls. Place in small roaster
or casserole. Pour soup over balls
and bake uncovered 35 minutes
at 400°. Cover. Bake 35 minutes longer.

CHICKEN CASSEROLE

Chub tells me this is a great dish to make use of leftovers—leftover chicken, rice, vegetables, whatever you find on hand. And before baking, it's best to mix them all together and let them sit overnight or all day in the refrigerator—"Let them ruminate and get friendly with each other." Then top with crumpled potato chips and bake. Of course, you can hardly go wrong with a topping of potato chips, whatever the dish. Adds some crunch. One of those fix-all things, like duct tape.

Ingredients
1 c. cooked chicken
1 c. cooked rice
¾ c. celery, chopped
1 t lemon juice
1 T chopped onion
¼ c. slivered almonds
½ c. mayonnaise
1 can cream of mushroom soup
½ t of salt
2 hard boiled eggs, chopped

Method
Mix all ingredients. Refrigerate overnight **or** all day. Top with crushed potato chips.
    Bake for 50 minutes at 350°.
    Makes 6 servings.

Chicken Casserole   6 servings

1 C cooked Chicken   Mix all ingredients.
1 C cooked rice   Refrigerate overnight or
¾ C Celery, Chopped   all day.
1 t   lemon juice   Top with Crushed potato Chips
1 T   Chopped onion
¼ C. slivered almonds   Bake for 50 minutes
½ C Mayonnaise   at 350°.
1 Can Cream of Mushroom Soup.
½ t. of salt
2 hard boiled eggs Chopped

CHILI CON CARNE

The garlic here is on a toothpick because, "You don't want to lose it." Chub explains: "On the farm we never used garlic. Garlic is Italian or Middle European. It's not English, or Scotch, or Irish. It wasn't in our manner of things." Sometimes I have the feeling she feels that way about me, too.

Ingredients and Method

Heat in a skillet 3 T (1½ T)* bacon fat or salad oil.

Add 1 onion (½) sliced

Cook 2 minutes. Add 1 lb. ground beef (½), 1 clove garlic on toothpick.

Cook and stir 15 min. Add 1 can red beans (½), 2 c. or more stewed, canned tomatoes or tomato sauce, 1 T (½) chili powder.

Simmer until thick (about 1 hour). Season to taste with salt and paprika.

Remove garlic.

(Serves 6)

---

* I assume Aunt Libby wrote these additional measurements in parentheses for reference for smaller batches, perhaps meant for one or two people instead of the family.

Chili con Carne

Heat in a skillet
     3 T (1½ T) bacon fat or salad oil

Add
     1 onion (½) sliced
Cook 2 min. Add
     1 lb ground beef (½)
     1 clove garlic on tooth pick
Cook and stir (5 min. Add
     1 can red beans (½)
     2 C. or more stewed, canned tomatoes or

tomato sauce
1 T (½) chili powder
Simmer until thick (about 1 hour). Season
To taste with salt and paprika
     Remove garlic   (Serves 6)

FRANK-CURRY BAKE

I would include this if only for the name. When I mention to Chub that I don't associate curry powder with Western Pennsylvania, she chuckles. "It's obvious this recipe didn't grow up in this neck of the woods." The Frank-Curry Bake also appears on a menu I found in Libby's collection.

Ingredients

¼ lb. wide noodles (2 c.)

1 c. sour cream

¾ to 1 tsp curry

½ t of salt

⅛ t pepper

5 franks

celery or poppy seeds

Method

Start heating over to 400°F.

Cook noodles as label directs, drain. Add sour cream, curry, salt, pepper. Toss lightly. Turn mixture into 10 x 6 x 2 cooking dish. Arrange frank on top. Sprinkle lightly with seeds. Bake 15 min or until heated through.

RECIPE for *Frank - Curry Bake*

from the kitchen of *Libby White*   <u>*Serves 2 or 3*</u>

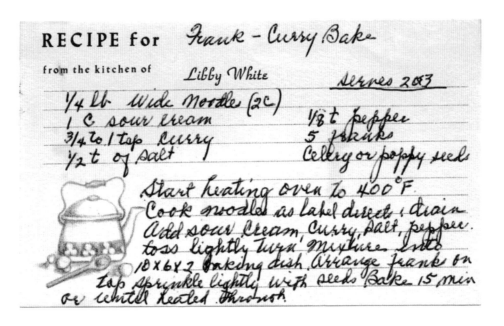

1/4 lb Wide Noodle (2 c)
1 C sour cream   1/8 t pepper
3/4 to 1 tsp Curry   5 franks
1/2 t of salt   Celery or poppy seeds

Start heating oven to 400°F.
Cook noodles as label direct, drain
Add sour cream, Curry, salt, pepper.
toss lightly Turn mixture into
10 x 6 x 2 baking dish. Arrange frank on
top sprinkle lightly with seeds Bake 15 min
or until heated through.

Menu - Mon. Sept 17. 1979

Frank - Curry Bake
3 bean - Salad - Muffins
Punch.
Devils Food Cake - Fruit

CREAMED POTATOES

"I never used this recipe but it sounds good," Chub says, reading it over. "It's one of your older recipes because it uses milk and flour instead of one of your cream soups. Cream of chicken, cream of mushroom, and so on and so forth. They sure do make it easier. Just not as good."

Ingredients
¼ c. minced onions (I use a little onion pwd*)
¼ c. butter
2 Tbs flour
½ t celery salt
pepper
2 c. milk (I don't use quite 2 c.)
2 c. diced cooked potatoes (often use more)
¼ c. chopped parsley

Method
Sauté onion in butter, blend in flour. Gradually add milk. Add fresh or dried parsley. Add potatoes and simmer. If dry parsley used, should simmer slowly for some time.

---

* powder

Creamed Potatoes.   Janet Laing
                                          1968
1/4 C Minced onion (I use a little onion pwd)
1/4 C butter
2 Tbs flour
1/2 t celery salt
Pepper
2 C milk (I don't use quite 2 C)
2 C diced cooked potatoes (often use more)
1/4 C chopped parsley
                    (over)

Sauté onion in butter, blend in
flour. Gradually add milk. Add
fresh or dried parsley. Add potatoes
and simmer. If dry parsley used
should simmer slowly for some
time.

THICK WHITE SAUCE

"Aunt Libby's own sauce," Chub says, "though it's typical of what we all did." She notes it calls for hot milk but she always used cold, "otherwise the sauce will go all lumpy on you." Today, many people use canned cream soups instead—mushroom, celery—but she always liked the real thing.

Ingredients
2 T butter
3 T flour
1 cup hot milk
½ t salt
⅛ t pepper
Special herbs and spice (optional)

Method
1. Melt butter in heavy sauce pan. Add flour; cook stirring constantly for 2 min, or until mixture known as roux is smooth and begins to bubble.
2. Remove sauce pan from heat. Add milk all at once. Return to heat: stir vigorously with wooden spoon or wire whisk. Sauce will be thickened and smooth in about 1 min.
3. Add salt and pepper. Cook over low heat for about 10 min. stirring occasionally.
4. Correct seasoning adding special herbs or spices, if desired.

Variations of White Sauce
For medium sauce, use 2 T flour and 1 T butter
> For thin sauce, use 1 T flour
> Curry sauce, add 1 t curry along with flour

Thick White Sauce
  2 T butter
  3 T flour
  1 cup hot milk
  ½ t salt
  ⅛ t pepper   Specials herb + spice (optional)
1. Melt butter in heavy sauce pan. Add
   flour; cook stirring constantly for
   2 min, or until mixture known as

roux is smooth and begins to bubble.
2. Remove sauce pan from heat. Add
   milk all at once. Return to heat;
   stir vigorously with wooden spoon
   or wire whisk. Sauce will be thickened
   and smooth in about 1 min.
3. Add salt and pepper. Cook over low heat
   for about 10 min, stirring occasionally.
4. Correct seasoning adding special herbs
   or spices if desired.

HAWAIIAN BEETS

"What's with all these recipes in here called 'Hawaiian' this or 'Tahitian' that?" I ask.

"That's just another way of saying there's pineapple in them," Chub explains with a look that says she wonders how her daughter ever married someone so naïve.

As for beets, they were a particular favorite of the family, though not necessarily the Hawaiian variety. "I suppose the pineapple gives them a little tanginess. If tanginess is what you're after," she says, like a woman who has had her fill of tanginess, thank you very much.

Ingredients
2 T butter
1 T flour or cornstarch
½ c. sugar
¼ t salt
¼ c. vinegar
¼ c. pineapple juice
¼ c. beet juice

Method
Cook juices with flour. Add beets #2 can and crushed pineapple or chunks (small can).

A Recipe From

Velma Ryburn
LIBBY WHITE

Hawaiian Beets

2 T. Butter
1 T Flour or cornstarch
½ C sugar
¼ t salt
¼ C. Vinegar
¼ C pineapple juice
¼ C beet juice

Cook juices with flour. Add beets #2 Can
& crushed pineapple or chunks (Sm. Can)

LIMA BAKE

"Oh wow!" says Chub, though I'm not sure why—she goes on to say that lima beans never went over that well at her house. When I say that I never knew anyone who *really* liked lima beans and wonder why anyone prepared them, she explains that lima beans were popular because they kept well and were a good substitute for potatoes "if you were looking for a starch." Like many recipes in Libby's collection, this was apparently copied from a cookbook—usually with personal touches added—either by herself or by someone else and given to her. "I never had anything against limas personally," Chub says, "but they had to be baby limas." She thinks a moment. "Baby limas. Yum."

Ingredients

1 c. dried limas

1 t salt

¼ c. chopped onion

¼ c. chopped green pepper

2 T cooking oil

1 c. cooked tomatoes

½ t or less of chili powder

shredded American cheese

Method

Mash beans; add 1 qt. of boiling water. Bring to a boil, cover and simmer about 1½ hours (add salt after 1st hour). Drain.

Cook onion and pepper in cooking oil until tender. Add tomatoes, chili p.*, and beans. Season to taste, salt and pepper. Pour into casserole. Sprinkle with cheese. Bake 350° about 25 minutes.

Makes 4 servings.

---

* powder

RECIPE for

from the kitchen of

From Bean Bag.
4 Servings

Lima Bake

1 C dried Limas	2 T Cooking oil
1 t Salt	1 C cooked tomatoes
1/4 C Chopped onion	1/2 t or less of Chili powder
1/4 C Chopped green pepper	Shredded American Cheese

Mash beans; Add 1 qt. of boiling Water
Bring to a boil, cover & simmer about
1 1/2 hrs (add salt after 1st hour) Drain
Cook onion + pepper in cooking oil until
tender. Add tomatoes, Chili p. + beans.
Season to taste, salt + pepper. Pour into Casserd
Sprinkle with Cheese Bake - 350° about 25 min.

ZUCCHINI-TUNA SALAD

"This sounds good," Chub offers. "That's interesting, putting the carrots in there too, that would add another flavor. Otherwise, a tuna salad can taste like . . . well, a tuna salad." Rather than use the tomatoes as a garnish, she'd quarter them and put them at the bottom of the serving dish, with scoops of the salad sitting on top.

"That would make a nice summer dish," she says.

"You know what they say, Chub," I put in. "Summer dishes and summer not."

Chub only sighs.

Ingredients
1 c. shredded zucchini
1 c. shredded carrots
1 can tuna, flaked
¾ c. mayonnaise
1 T sweet pickle chopped
1 t celery seed or chopped celery
1 T pickle juice
lettuce and tomato wedges

Method
Combine zu and car*. Drain tuna; mix lighting with zu mix until blended. Combine mayonnaise, pickle and juice and celery until blended. Add to other mix. Serve on lettuce. Garnish with tomatoes.

5–7 servings

---

* Zucchini and carrots, in case you didn't catch that.

Zucchini - tuna salad

1 C. shredded zucchini
1 C shredded carrots
1 Can tuna - flaked
3/4 C Mayonnaise
1 T sweet pickle chopped
1 t celery seed or Chopped celery
1 T pickle juice
Lettuce and tomato wedges

Combine zu & car. Drain
tuna; mix lightly with zu
mix until blended. Com-
bine mayonnaise. pickle.
and juice and celery until
blended. Add to other mix.
Serve on lettuce. garnish
with tomatoes.   5 - 7 serving

JELL-O SALAD

"The infamous Jell-O salad," I say.

Chub asks, "Why 'infamous?'"

I say, "Okay, ubiquitous, then."

Chub says, "You don't like Jell-O salads?"

I say, "I'm just saying it seems everybody has a Jell-O salad; they always take them to church functions."

Chub says, "I didn't think you went to many church functions."

I say, "I don't, I mean, I remember when I used to, when I was younger . . ."

Chub asks, "Was Jell-O salad the reason why you stopped going to church functions?"

Oh my.

Ingredients and Method

Heat 1¾ c. water to boiling and dissolve a 3 oz. package of fruit gelatin. Chill until slightly thick. Add the un-drained pineapple (8¾ oz. can, Dole), 1 c. of sour cream or cottage cheese, and ¼ c. of chopped nuts.

Jello – with Crushed Pineapple

   Heat 1¾ C water to boiling and
dissolve a 3 oz. package of Fruit gelatin.
Chill until slightly thick. Add the un-
drained pineapple (8¾ oz. – can – Dole)
1 C. of sour cream or cottage cheese
and ¼ C. of chopped nuts.

PUMPKIN TEA BREAD

Chub recognizes this as one of her recipes: "I made this while I was doing a lot of zucchini stuff. A long time ago. Zucchini doesn't have much flavor of its own, it picks up the flavor of whatever else is with it."

Then why do you put zucchini in things? seems a logical question.

"It adds body to what you're making."

"I'm learning something," I say.

"Most of this is just common sense," she says.

Ingredients

1 c. pumpkin	2 c. flour
1 c. grated zucchini	1 tsp baking soda
¾ c. sugar	½ tsp. baking powder
2 eggs	2 tsp. of cinnamon
¼ c. oil	¼ tsp. salt
¼ c. melted butter or oleo	½ c. chopped pecans or walnuts

Method

Preheat oven to 350°F. In large bowl, combine pumpkin, zucchini, sugar, eggs, oil, and margarine; mix well. In separate bowl, combine flour, b. soda, b. powder, cinn., and salt. Add dry ingredients to pumpkin mixture; mix only till flour is moistened. Stir in nuts.

Spoon into well greased 9 x 5 x 3" loaf pan. Bake 60 min. or till pick comes out clean. Cool 10 minutes; remove from pan.

Yield: 1 loaf.

Cheese Filling

1 (3 oz.) package cr.* cheese beaten with softened 3 T oleo or butter. Beat till fluffy. Spread between slices of tea bread.

---

* Cream

Pumpkin Tea Bread

1 c. pumpkin   2 c. flour
1 c. grated zucchini   1 tsp. baking soda
3/4 c. sugar   1/3 tsp. " powder
2 eggs   1/2 tsp. gr. cinnamon
1/4 c. oil   1/4 tsp. salt.
1/4 c. melted butter or oleo.   1/2 c. chopped pecans
                                                       or walnuts.
       Preheat oven to 350°F.   In large bowl,
combine pumpkin, zucchini, sugar, eggs,

oil & margarine; mix well. In separate
bowl, combine flour, b. soda, b. powder,
cinn. & salt. Add dry ingredients to
pumpkin mixture; mix only till
flour is moistened. Stir in nuts.
       Spoon into well greased 9 x 5 x 3" loaf pan.
Bake 60 min. or till pick comes out clean.
Cool 10 min.; remove from pan. Yield: 1 loaf.

Cheese filling: 1 (3 oz) pkg. cr cheese beaten with 3 T. oleo or butter
                                                            softened
        Beat till fluffy. Spread between slices of Tea Bread.

LEMON PIE

"This is a basic," Chub says, "and the old-fashioned way. It's not just using lemon pudding or anything like that—this is the real thing. Real lemons. That would be pretty radical, in this day and age. It's probably Aunt Helen's recipe, that's where Libby got it. Aunt Helen was the real thing, too."

Ingredients
½ c. milk
Grated **rind** and **juice** of 2 lemons
¼ c. melted butter
1 T cornmeal
2 c. sugar
4 eggs
dash of salt

Method
1. Preheat oven to 375°.
2. Grease 8-inch pie plate; dust with flour; line with pastry.
3. In mixing bowl, combine milk, lemon juice and rind and butter.
4. In bowl of electric mixer, combine 1 T flour, cornmeal, sugar, eggs, salt. Beat until well blended. Gradually beat in lemon mixture.
5. Pour into pastry. Bake 40–45 min.

A Recipe From   LIBBY WHITE

Lemon Pie

½ C. milk
Grated rind + juice of 2 lemon
¼ C melted butter
1 T cornmeal
2 C sugar
4 eggs
Dash of salt.

It browns on top.

1. Preheat oven to 375°
2. Grease 8-inch pie plate; dust with flour; line with pastry
3. In mixing bowl combine milk, lemon juice + rind + butter
4. In bowl of electric mixer combine 1 T flour, corn meal, sugar, eggs, salt. Beat until well blended. Gradually beat in lemon mixture
5. Pour into pastry. Bake 40-45 min.

RINK-TUM-DITTY

No one seems to know where the name comes from, but cookbooks from New England to Arizona to the Hickory Women's Club seem anxious to claim it as a particular regional favorite. Some consider it a version of Welsh rarebit with tomatoes or tomato soup replacing the beer, to be served on toast or crackers, though this recipe is noticeably plain. When Chub reads it over, her pronouncement is, "It's a glorified version of scrambled eggs" and tosses it to the side of the table.

Ingredients and Method
2 onions diced and cooked slowly in 2 tbsps. butter. Melt 1–2 lb. cheese in pain over low fire. Add onions to cheese, then add 3 beaten eggs and 1 cup of milk and cook slowly until thick. Serve immediately on toasted bread or crackers. Garnish with paprika if you like.

Rink-Tum-Ditty

2 onions diced and cooked slowly in 2 tbsps. butter. Melt 1-2 lb. cheese in pan over low fire. Add onions to cheese, then add 3 beaten eggs and 1 cup of milk and cook slowly until thick. Serve immediately on toasted bread or crackers. Garnish with paprika, if you like.

"And so on and so forth," Chub says. A phrase she uses when she has nothing more to say on a subject. It is apparent that this segment of looking through recipes is drawing to a close.

"So, were you a better cook than Aunt Libby?" I ask, trying to get a rise out of her. But Chub considers her answer carefully.

"I don't know if she ever had the chance to be a good cook. She collected recipes, that's where all these come from. But these are all recipes from other people, not recipes that she developed herself. In reality, Libby and Jessie, they were two old maids, cooking old maid meals for each other."

Chub shrugs her regrets and closes the recipe box, effectively putting a lid on the subject.

Recipes

THE
THINGS THEY
USED

....

Part 2

NUTMEG GRATER

This kitchen thing bears an uncanny resemblance, only smaller, to a coffin or some ancient mummy case. Or maybe one of those spiked cabinets used for torture in the Inquisition. All these dire associations brought on by a harmless little nutmeg grater.

Actually, it's rather clever, or at least functional. You scrape the nutmeg across the grater; the grated nutmeg falls through the holes into the base for handy storage. Neat. Nutmeg is a spice that is tied, at least in my experience, to the holiday season, or at least to the wintertime—something to sprinkle over eggnog and mulled wine or the custardy pies and puddings that appear at this time of year. Botanically known as *Myristica fragans*, the nutmeg tree is an evergreen indigenous to the Spice Islands in Indonesia, though in the 1600s a Frenchman named Pierre Poivre (literally, Peter Piper) smuggled seeds that spread the cultivation to islands off East Africa and eventually to the Caribbean. At one time, nutmeg was one of the world's most valuable and coveted spices; wars were fought over its trade, people massacred and enslaved to control its production. Used in sweet as well as savory dishes, nutmeg is found in the cuisines of India, Greece, the Middle East, and Japan as well as Europe. The nutmeg tree also produces another spice, mace, which has a more delicate flavor.

Besides its flavor, nutmeg was prized for centuries, particularly in Europe, as a preservative and for having or giving magical powers. Nutmeg was credited for warding off the plague; one monk in the sixteenth century advised young men to rub it on their genitals for virility; tucking a nutmeg into the left armpit before social events was said to attract admirers. (Hmm, maybe I should try that—the nutmeg-in-the-armpit thing, not the . . .) Nutmeg can indeed get you high in large quantities (I mean large, six or eight teaspoons worth), but it can also cause convulsions, palpitations, nausea, dehydration, and generalized body pain. The *Myristica* of its official name comes from myristicin, an oil classified as a "deliriant." Maybe that's why I'm deliriously happy eating Marty's pumpkin pie, laced with nutmeg and cinnamon. Delirious enough, perhaps, to see nutmeg graters as small mummy cases. . . .

NUTMEG GRATER

To judge by the number of antique nutmeg graters in my reference books—there are six pages worth in the fifth edition of *300 Years of Kitchen Collectibles* by Linda Campbell Franklin—or the number I see laid out on the tables of flea markets and antique fairs, you'd think that Americans come from generations of nutmeg-grating devotees. But as Franklin notes in one entry, by 1890 there was apparently only one manufacturer of nutmeg graters. She goes on to say, "I suppose by that time, powdered nutmeg in tins had pretty much obviated the need for graters."

A curious thing happened as technology worked its way into every aspect of our everyday lives and processed food became more prevalent: people started to prefer the prepared and packaged food to fresh. And it wasn't all just for the convenience. For Americans at least, it became a mark of being modern and up-to-date—and more than that, too: it became an indication of affluence and success—to open a can of peas or tomatoes or asparagus rather than deal with vegetables right from the ground. I grew up suspicious of anything that didn't come from the sealed goodness of a package.

In the Sixties when hippies advocated "back to nature," few people appeared to listen. But eventually the message—at least in regard to food—seeped through the layers of American tastes and mores. Of course, the general hedonism of the Eighties and Nineties—with its growth industry of TV cooking shows—certainly didn't hurt. Whatever . . . the fact is that fresh simply tastes better. Surprise! Today it's become fashionable to tout such qualities as Farm-Fresh and Locally Grown, and our diets and taste buds are all better off for it. I've even been known—*Gasp*!—to frequent farmers' markets. Roadside vegetable stands. Community gardens. What is the world coming to?

NUT CHOPPER

"Does this image make you think of anything?"

"How do you mean?"

"Well, with some of the kitchen things, you said they reminded you of other things. . . ."

"A cat toy."

"Be serious."

"I am serious. A cat would love that ball on the top, batting it back and forth."

"Except the rod isn't flexible, it's rigid. It's a nut chopper."

"I can see it's a nut chopper, silly."

"What about some stories of you and your sister chopping nuts for holiday baking. . . ."

"My sister was allergic to nuts so we never included them in anything."

"You know what I mean."

"I think chopping nuts is one of those things like nutmeg. Most of the time, people buy their ingredients already chopped or ground or however they're going to use them. People just don't have time nowadays. I know I see nut choppers around, but I've never known anyone to use one."

"You're not being much help."

"Sorry. Isn't it enough for a photograph just to show a thing as it is? At least, that's what you always say. It's a beautiful picture of a nut chopper. What more can a poor nut chopper expect?"

"That's fine if you're only doing illustration, otherwise there needs to be additional levels. . . ."

"Okay. Well, it's a festive little thing, its tassel waving in the air. That's one thing I'll say about it, you'd have way too much fun using it. I can see you flailing away at it. A chopping fool."

"Thanks. I think."

"Chop, chop, chop, chop, chop!" Marty whacks an imaginary plunger up and down a number of times, then stops, unscrews an imaginary lid, looks inside, then looks at me. "Ah, nuts!"

BUNCH O' KNIVES

Why are these knives tied together? The truth is I know as little about these knives as you do. Maybe they came from Marty's family farm near Hickory, Pennsylvania; maybe they came from my own family's house in Beaver Falls; or maybe I picked them up at one of the flea markets or antique fairs I scour to find these objects that speak to me. That let me know they have a story to tell.

History is all about stories. It's hearsay and speculations about events in times past. Even eyewitness accounts are suspect—as demonstrated by any police report involving multiple witnesses. But artifacts—objects made or modified by people—are witnesses from the past that are present in the here and now, and the stories they tell are objective. To unlock the messages from artifacts, cultural archeologists excavate layers of meaning from material culture. In regard to these knives, such a dig would consider the manufacturer, consulting pattern books to establish when they were made and where they were sold. That could tell us something of the social stratum of which they were part. Scientists would study the materials from which the knives were made—for instance if they're silver or silverplate—and they would determine how often the knives were used, which would tell us if they were everyday flatware or saved for special occasions. The patina would be studied to isolate the environment where the knives were stored, which would tell us if they continued to be used after the original owners or if they were stored away as keepsakes. Or maybe just forgotten in a drawer. It would be noted that the string appears to be from a more recent era than the knives.

But I think the knives in this image have another story to tell, as well. A story of a different order. In the process of becoming the subject of a photograph, these knives talk to us of holding on to the past. Of memories of family dinners and holiday gatherings. Of people we have known from another era, parents or grandparents, whom we have loved and lost. Of things put away. Of time gone forever. Stories infinitely less precise than scientific inquiries. But, without disparaging those efforts, resonating deeper.

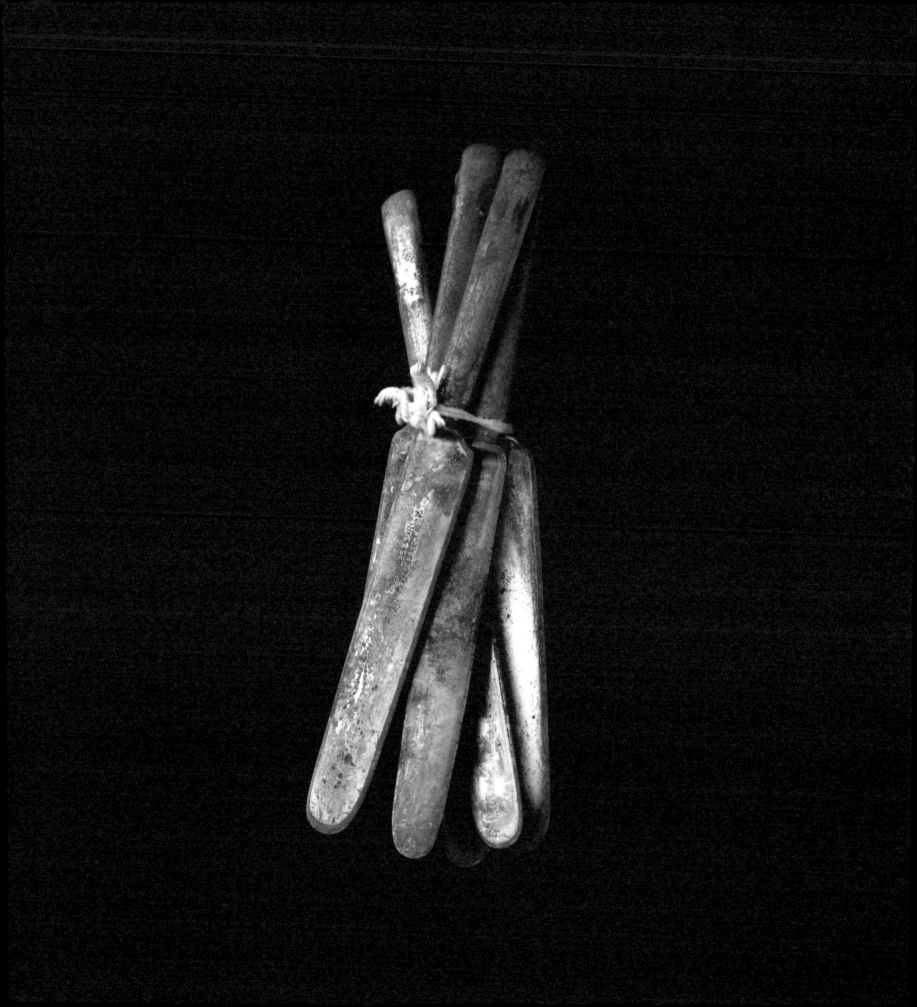

POPCORN POPPER

Speaking of family gatherings. There's the image of the family sitting around the fireplace—or in my case, standing around the stove in the kitchen—popping popcorn in a popcorn popper.

"Did that really happen?" Marty says.

"I remember we tried it once with one of these things. But most of the popcorn didn't pop, and the rest was either burnt or tasted like it. Maybe we were just inept popcorn poppers."

Popcorn has been around for more than five thousand years—in the Americas, of course, because that's where corn was. Zapotecs and Aztecs not only ate popcorn, but also used it for necklaces and to decorate headdresses. Christopher Columbus noted that Indians sold popcorn to his crew (for the show?); there's reason to believe that when the Indians came to Thanksgiving dinner at Plymouth in 1621, they brought popcorn. Colonists loved popcorn with cream and sugar for breakfast. Popcorn carts were seen on street corners after they were invented in 1885; home versions were invented in 1925. During the Depression, popcorn was one of the few treats most people could afford; during World War II, with sugar rationed, popcorn was one of the few treats most people could find.

Popcorn was first cooked by throwing kernels on a hot rock; part of the fun was catching the popped corn as it flew off in all directions. Today, there are hot air poppers with computers to measure heat, salt, and butter. In the industry, popped kernels are called flakes and come in two shapes, either butterfly or mushroom. Unpopped kernels are known, rather unkindly I'd say, as old maids. There are generally two reasons why kernels don't pop: moisture or a leaky hull.

"When I was growing up," Marty says, "popcorn came in a tin plate with an aluminum foil cover that popped up like a chef's hat when you put it on the stove. It was great fun to poke it into different shapes. You know, all this is making me hungry." She takes a packet from the cupboard and puts it in the microwave. Instant popcorn!

And I didn't even mention this popper reminds me of a stylized crocodile. Or a man trap.

DOUBLE BROILER

Or this cozy scene: A cold winter's morning, the milk bottles from the back porch stretching their necks with the frozen cream pushing up the cardboard caps, Mom standing at the kitchen stove spooning up fresh-made oatmeal or Cream of Wheat from a white-enamel double boiler.

"Given what you've said so far, I'm afraid to think what could be wrong with this picture."

"Nothing, actually, except it's not a memory. My mother never took the time to make the long kind of either cereal, and she didn't have or use a double boiler. She would do the instant kind in a sauce pan. Then we couldn't have it again for a couple of days afterward because it took that long for the remains in the pan to soak clean after sitting in soapy water in the sink. I grew to really appreciate the convenience of Wheaties and Cheerios."

A double boiler is the Americanized, no-nonsense version of a time-honored utensil the French call a *bain-marie*—Mary's Bath—named supposedly for Mary the Jewess, an ancient alchemist who first developed the technique to heat metals. In cooking, it is used for heating anything that needs steady heat so it won't burn, such as thick sauces like Hollandaise and *beurre blanc*, and of course porridge-like cereals. The device is an exercise in constants: once the water in the lower, larger half reaches the boiling point, it can't get hotter so both halves remain at a steady heat. Nifty.

"So tell me a story about the Legendary Chub and her double boiler."

"There aren't any," Marty says. "I asked Mom. She never remembers seeing one being used when she was growing up. And the only time she used one later was to melt chocolate for baking."

"But I found this one in her basement at the farm. And it certainly looks used."

"Oh, it was undoubtedly used. It's like I said, Great Aunt Mary E wouldn't let anyone near the kitchen. When Mom got married, she literally couldn't boil water; she had never seen it done."

The Legendary Chub? Unable to boil water? Oh my. It's like learning the Oracle of Delphi couldn't tell the Greeks from the Persians. . . .

SYRUP PITCHER

As long as we're talking about breakfasts and cold snowy mornings, we can't forget pancakes—particularly buckwheat pancakes, though the real thing is hard to find—with maple syrup. Something else, incidentally, that is often hard to find as the genuine article.

Maple syrup, like corn, is one of the few foods that originated in the Americas, not brought here from somewhere else. No one knows when the aboriginal Indians in the northeastern part of North America discovered that the watery stuff seeping from certain trees at a certain time of year was actually tasty, but sweetwater, as they called it, was around when the first Europeans waded ashore. Essentially, maple syrup is sap from maple trees that has been boiled down until the water in it evaporates and what is left is thick and, well, syrupy. That's it in theory, but actually doing it is a time-intensive process that takes a lot of work.

Work, acerbated by the fact that the sugar season, as it is known, starts in mid-February when there's a lot of snow on the ground, and lasts only four to six weeks. Moreover, not any ol' maple tree secretes the right sap. As might be expected, sugar maples are prime, along with red maples, black maples, and occasionally silver maples. (What's left? Well, you want to stay away from big leaf maples, Manitoba maples, and striped maples for starters.) Trees need to be thirty to forty years of age before they can be tapped, and each tree can usually take only between one and three taps depending on the tree's diameter. A grove of trees is called a sugar bush; the building where the sap is boiled is called a sugar shack. Technological advances include plastic tubing instead of buckets, vacuum pumps, and reverse-osmosis machines. Canada, the United States, and Vermont each have their own grading standards, ranging from light (mild) to dark (molasses-like).

This dispenser held syrup for years on the counter of The Shantee, the restaurant attached to Marty's family's farm, but now is relegated, in this calorie- and carbohydrate-conscious household, to holding dishwashing liquid on our kitchen sink. As far as I can tell, it doesn't seem to mind.

PITCHER WITH CHICKENS

Marty looks up, perturbed at the interruption, from her cooking magazine. "Go ahead."

I know that look. Usually I just give up and go away. But I figure it's now or never.

"Tell me a maple syrup story from the farm."

She leans back in her chair at the table, one arm thrown over the back. Resigned to her fate.

"They never made maple syrup, if that's what you mean. I only remember Grandpap White putting syrup on everything he ate."

"Everything?"

"Everything. Eggs, ham, porridge, corn, lettuce, beefheart—" At my look, she continues. "Grandpap believed in eating everything of a cow. Heart, tongue, brains . . . Sunday dinners were sometimes awful." She shudders at the memory before continuing. "You know that pitcher with the chickens on it? It always sat on the table with syrup in it. Log cabin—it had to be Log Cabin."

"Named, by the way, for the story of Abraham Lincoln being born in same." Her steady, I've-got-you-in-my-sights look tells me it's probably not the time to also mention that what Grandpap spread on his food wasn't actually maple syrup—it is one of several popular less expensive substitutes, some with only maple flavoring. But of course I can't let things go without aiming back.

"Always on the table? You mean all day. . . ."

"Always."

"Wouldn't it collect dust? Bugs?"

She considers. "Well, I don't remember them ever cleaning it out. Just adding more to it."

"On the other hand, if he smothered everything with syrup, he probably couldn't taste anything he ate anyway. A few flies and gnats would just add some protein to the mix."

She weighs her weapon in her mind, then uncocks the hammer and returns to her cooking magazine. In her pursuit to make food for us that doesn't require being smothered in anything.

BACON FLATTENER

As long as we're blowing the diet by adding calories with pancakes smothered (there's no other way) in (real) maple syrup, we might as well clog up the arteries a bit with bacon fat.

This totally functional and rather superfluous cast-iron utensil, complete with the bas-relief image that I'm willing to wager is of the Three Little Pigs, goes by the official name of the Bacon Press. The fact is, you can find beef bacon, chicken bacon, turkey bacon, lamb bacon, goat bacon, even vegetarian bacon, but as all Americans know, they aren't really bacon. What you may not know is that in the United States, our bacon is almost always made from pork bellies, which, given American's bacon mania, explains why pork bellies are so important on the commodities market. Other countries, whose bacon is made from cuts of the leaner side or back of a pig, shake their collective heads at American's penchant for bacon that comes from the streaky fatty underbellies. I suppose it's understandable, given that America was built on the right to be contrary and do what's not necessarily good for us. In response to our fat-conscious society, pork raised today is 50 percent leaner than it was just twenty years ago. Still, that doesn't explain bacon ice cream, bacon-infused vodka, bacon donuts, bacon mints, chicken-fried bacon, and—wait for it—chocolate-covered bacon.

Bacon is differentiated from ham or salt pork by the brine used to cure it. Among the ingredients in bacon brine is sodium nitrate, a preservative that's thought to increase the risk of heart disease and diabetes. Yes, there is nitrate-free bacon, and cooking bacon at lower temperatures or in a microwave can help prevent deadly nitrosamine from forming, but you still have to deal with 1,262 milligrams of sodium in two raw slices of bacon. Maybe the culprit lies, as Arun Gupta says, that bacon possesses six types of umami, which elicit an addictive neurochemical response; or maybe it's just in our national character—as early as 1708, satirist Ebenezer Cooke complained that practically all American food was infused with bacon.

Whatever. I talked about bacon enough that Marty is currently cooking up a skillet-full, using this bacon press to flatten the curly little devils.

DIPPER

"Great Aunt Mary E's ladle?"

"Actually, it's a dipper for the drinking water."

"As opposed to . . .?"

"They kept it with the pail on the back porch."

"Pail? You're losing me."

"My grandparents kept a pail of water on the back porch with drinking water."

"Why didn't they use the tap? Or was it one of those small hand pumps beside the sink?"

"No, they had running water. But the cistern was up the hill at the barn. It ran *really* slow; it could take hours to fill a bucket. So they brought up drinking water from the springhouse."

"Springhouse?"

Marty looks at her hopelessly naïve, city-born and -bred husband. "There was a springhouse built into the bank down at the creek. The water was always cool and fresh, so somebody—usually Grandpap—brought up a pail of water every day. They kept it on the back porch for drinking. And this was probably the dipper they kept with it."

"Probably?"

"Well, when there were field hands, they kept another bucket of drinking water outside for them as well."

"And another dipper."

"Well, yes. They never wanted us to drink from the one the field hands used. Most of the time they were hobos; they got off the train at the junction and slept in the barn. We weren't allowed to go near the barn either. They told us we might get polio or TB or something."

For once, this hopelessly naïve, city-born and -bred husband at least knows when it's best to keep his mouth shut.

ICE CUBE TRAY

Each year there are a number of sounds that help announce the arrival of warmer weather, the coming of hot summer days. The *ffft-ffft-ffft-ffft-ffft* of a lawn sprinkler. A metal hose nozzle dropped on concrete. A ball bounced repeatedly against a wall. The *flip-flop* of flip-flops. And for some of us of a certain age, the small creaks and groans of the separator in a metal ice cube tray as it is pulled open, the crackle of the ice and the jingle of the separator as it is pulled free.

Ice. A mystery all its own. For one thing, ice is the only known non-metallic substance to expand when it freezes. For another, ice is on the top. Almost all other substances are heavier and denser as solids than as liquids, but ice is about 9 percent lighter than the water from which it is frozen. Drop ice into water and it floats; try that with another solid. The reason is that on the molecular level, there is a hole at the heart of the submicroscopic hexagonal pattern of an ice crystal. It's a good thing, actually. Otherwise, oceans and lakes would freeze from the bottom up, making melting quite difficult. Which means aquatic life would not only *not* survive, but human life itself would never have evolved in the first place. Let's hear it for ice!

Refrigeration, which led to the ability to make ice at home, was used commercially in the United States by the late 1800s for brewing and meat processing, but the systems utilized toxic gas that occasionally leaked—not what you want chugging away in the corner of your kitchen. With the discovery of non-flammable, non-toxic refrigerants such as Freon, household refrigerators became possible in 1915, though the machinery had to be in another room. In 1923, Frigidaire introduced the first self-contained unit, but the first refrigerator to gain widespread use was General Electric's Monitor-Top, so-named because the motor on top looked like the Civil War ironclad warship. As early as 1916, refrigerators had compartments for ice cube trays, and a major innovation in the 1950s and '60s was automatic ice making. About the same time, plastic trays replaced the old metal variety, though extricating the cubes from one always makes me think I'm wringing its neck.

ICE PICK

It is understandable if this particular utensil is mistaken for an awl. Such as a Bradawl or Scratch Awl used in woodworking—the Bradawl for making an indentation in wood or similar materials to ease the placement of a nail or screw; the Scratch Awl to scribe a line for a hand saw or chisel to follow. Or it could be mistaken for a Stitching Awl, used in sewing heavy materials such as leather or canvas. No, the fact is it's a kitchen tool, though one that most of my generation never had cause to use, and that younger generations have heard about but have never seen. An ice pick.

An ice pick was a common and necessary household tool used to trim and shape a block of ice to fit in an ice box. Which, of course, brings up a related subject that most people nowadays have only heard about. An icebox was just that: a cabinet for home refrigeration, the walls of which were insulated with materials such as cork or sawdust, and a compartment made of tin or zinc to hold a large block of ice. Once the ice melted—which, by the way, required a drip pan underneath that needed emptying once a day or so—a new block of ice had to be delivered. This gave rise to the name, though not necessarily the action, of Eugene O'Neill's play, *The Iceman Cometh*. It is interesting to note that Consumers Union made its first and only test of iceboxes in 1937. The industry tried to forestall the inevitable march of progress and technology by claiming that only an icebox could keep food "properly humidified" and eliminate refrigerant gasses that "taint the food." However, by the 1940s and 1950s, iceboxes for the most part were replaced by electric and even gas refrigerators, though you still hear older people (yours truly) refer to them by the older name.

The first and only time I actually used an ice pick was when I had my first apartment as a college student. Unaware that refrigerators occasionally need to be defrosted, the freezer compartment eventually iced up so completely that the opening was only a slit. The landlord, a man with a profound lack of a sense of humor, pulled the plug and handed me said tool. "Here you go. And if you poke a hole in the coils, you owe me a new icebox."

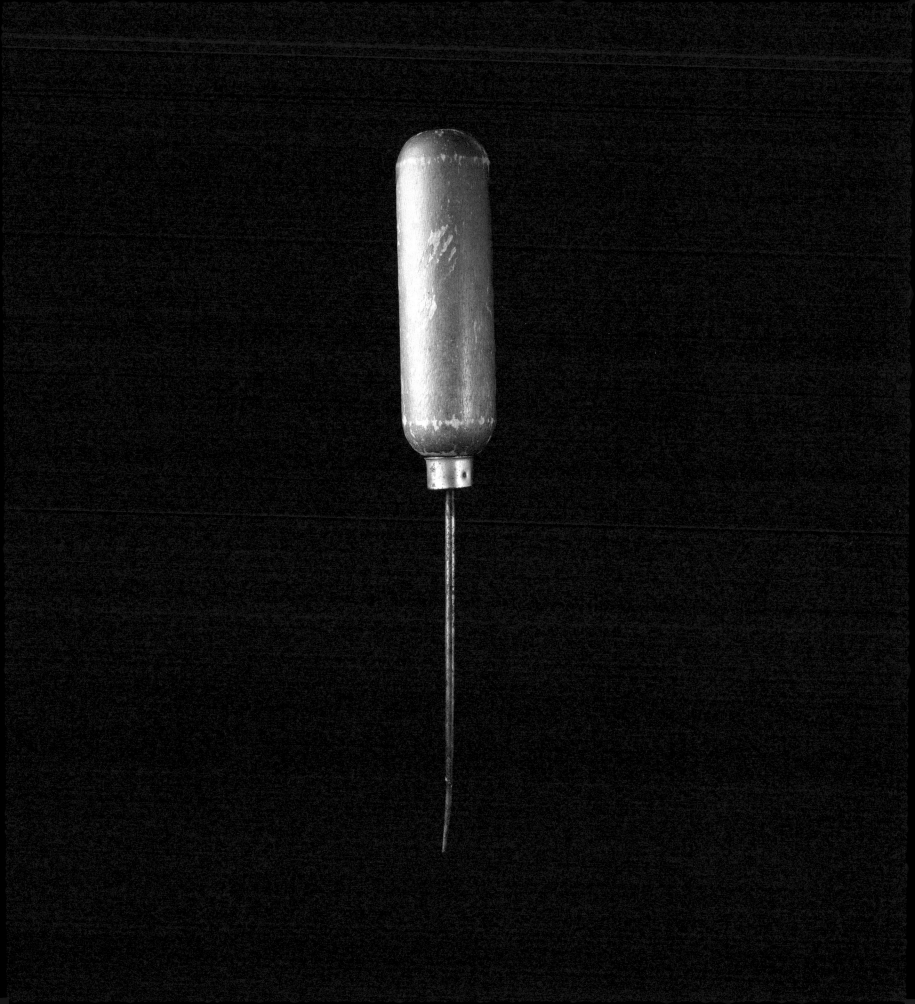

ICE TONGS

"My father was an ice man."

"You always said he was cold," Marty says.

"No, I mean he was actually an ice man. When he was in high school, he worked on an ice wagon in town. His father, ol' Doc Snodgrass, thought it might help toughen him up. The crews had to fight at the ice house for the best blocks of ice. I guess it got pretty rough. I think the good doctor was trying to make up for my grandmother, who let my father's hair grow into long tresses and dressed him as a girl till he was eight years old."

"That's awful."

"The blocks of ice could weigh up to a hundred pounds or more. You had to learn how to swing it up on your shoulder just right so you could carry it into a house and put it in the icebox. Father said it was all a matter of balance."

"Sounds like he had to learn how to balance a lot of things in his life. So, when you look at this image of a pair of ice tongs, what do you see?"

"Well, first of all I see it as a graceful tool. And yes, it reminds me of my father, that's undoubtedly why I told you that story. And then other things kick in, like metaphor. I'm reminded of somebody trying to cover their modesty, which is rather comic. And it sort of reminds me of a dancer doing a buck and wing, too. It's complicated."

"I guess it is."

"The point is, that's how we see everything. In a mixture of perceptions. Function and form, memory and metaphor. It's just that some things, some images, are more evocative than others. I think that's when and where art comes in. In those levels."

She picks up the tongs and walks them across the tabletop, then lifts one tong leg and waves it at me. "Wouldn't this look great on the wall of the kitchen?"

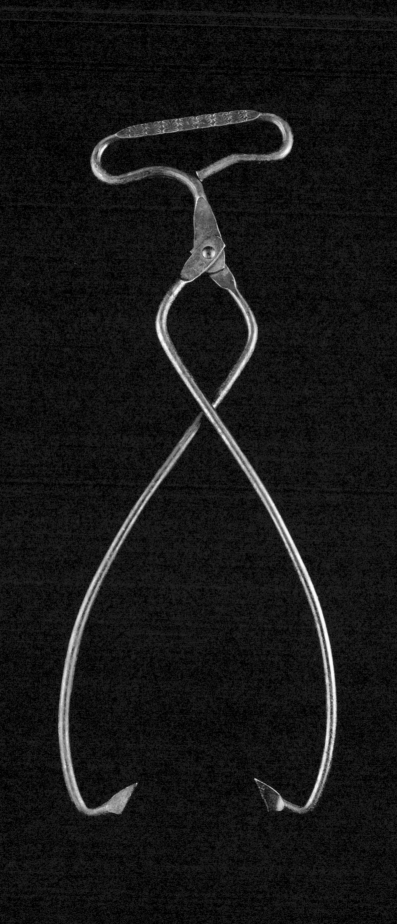

WATER BOTTLE

"Okay, your turn. What do you see in this picture?"

"A refrigerator water bottle."

"Well, of course. But I mean like we were talking about? Do you see anything more?"

"You mean like a metaphor or something? Not really."

"Give it a shot."

Marty squints at it in pseudo concentration. You'd think I'd learn. "It's got really broad shoulders. Like a linebacker. It's the Jack Lambert of water bottles. And it's wearing a dickey, a ruffled one, all the way down to its little glass toes."

"You're being silly."

Marty bats her eyes, as if to say, *Little ol' me?*

"What about memories? Does it bring back any memories?"

She shrugs. "As a matter of fact, Grandpap always kept a bottle like this in the fridge."

"What about the pail of water from the springhouse?"

"Different Grandpap. That was Grandpap White. This is Grandpap Beard."

"Anything else you remember about it?"

"He always drank from it when he came in from gardening or cutting the grass. I'm afraid that's all I remember. I never liked it because it was too slippery and hard to hold."

"That's a pretty subjective criticism."

"I thought that's what you wanted: a subjective response." She pumps her shoulders. *What?*

"What about design? Do you have any associations with Art Deco?"

"Not really. To me Art Deco nowadays is sort of Funky-Retro."

"Sort of like me."

She looks through me as if through a glass bottle. With a ruffled dickey down to my toes.

MECHANICAL ICE CREAM SCOOP

It's curious that the mechanical ice cream disher was invented before the simpler ice cream scoop, but such is the case. The mechanical disher is credited to Alfred L. Cralle, an African American born in Virginia in 1866. After working as a carpenter with his father, where he showed an interest in mechanics, he attended several schools founded by the American Baptist Home Mission Society to help educate African Americans after the Civil War. Eventually he settled in Pittsburgh, Pennsylvania, where he worked in a drug store and as a porter at the St. Charles Hotel. A testament, no doubt, that even with an education, a black man at the time had trouble finding a job worthy of his skills.

But the society of the day couldn't keep the man from thinking. While working at the St. Charles, he observed that ice cream, which had become very popular, was hard to dispense. The stuff tended to stick to spoons and ladles used to dish it out, and usually required two hands and a like number of utensils to serve it. Accordingly, he came up with a device he called an Ice Cream Mold and Disher, which cleared the inside of ice cream and other foods if they got stuck and could be operated with one hand. The thirty-year-old Cralle was granted his patent for the device in 1897.

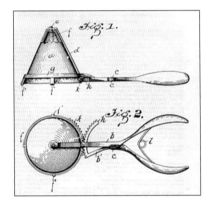

Though a number of similar devices were patented around this time, Cralle's basic design stuck. However, though he eventually became a successful businessman, he was unheralded as the inventor of the ice cream scoop in his own day. Also, he never received the credit he deserves in coming up with a utensil that is one of the most fun to use in the kitchen.

APPLE PEELER

It's only human to be tempted by The Allure of the Latest Contraption. To fall for the charms of the newest thing, to the extent that we lose sight of why we thought the thing was useful in the first place. Take, for instance, this apple parer, one of the first machines complete with gears and springs to find its way into the kitchen. Source books for collecting such things list dozens of variations, starting as early as 1803. The problem with such an apparatus is that it requires an apple of perfect proportion, aligned to within a millimeter of its axis, for the blessed thing to be most effective. Otherwise, you scrape off as much of the flesh as you do of the peel to get the apple reasonably denuded. Wasteful, no matter how you slice it. Of course, that's easy for me to say; I'm not the one a couple of centuries ago who was faced with bushels upon bushels of apples to pare.

Like most of us, the apple isn't native to America, yet it's at the core of much of our iconography (sorry, I couldn't resist). American as Apple Pie takes its meaning from the apple, not the pie. Johnny Appleseed is a true American hero, as much for his altruism as for his trees. Everyone knows that an apple a day keeps the doctor away; that she's the apple of my eye; and that so-and-so is a bad apple. You should never compare apples to oranges. The center of our culture, New York City, is the Big Apple, or just The Apple. It wouldn't be the same if it were called The Pear. Or The Kumquat.

So, what is the attraction of such a mechanical device, even when it proves impractical? Perhaps it is the recognition of another mind at work. Our brains hunger for stimulation the way we crave—well, a cinnamon-y apple cobbler or other tasty treat. Indeed, an apple parer is a marvel of ingenuity and problem-solving. Not only does the apple have to spin, but the blade needs to maintain its bite as it whirls around the length of the fruit. Fascinating. Like an astrolabe with teeth, appealing in its orbits.

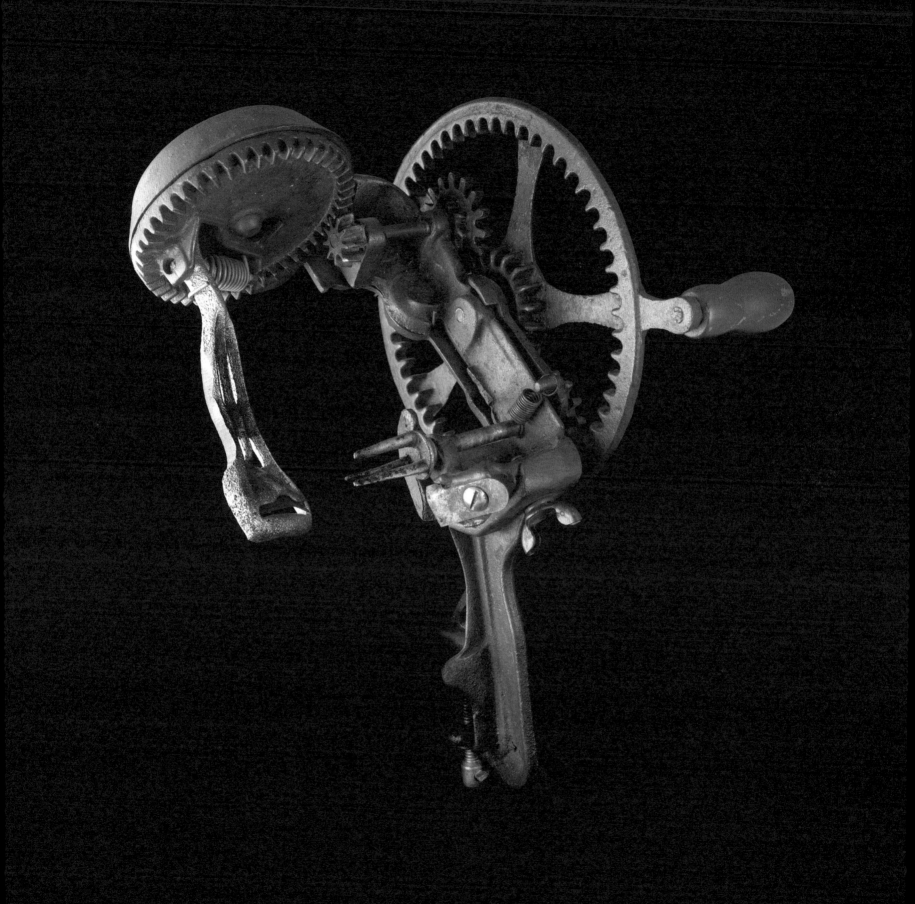

CHERRY PITTER

Seeing is believing, or so goes the adage. Well, when it comes to photographs, Photoshop pretty much gives that the lie. But the adage was in trouble before software made it possible to alter a photograph's take on reality. For instance, just because the fellow in this image looks rather insect-like, or possibly reptilian, doesn't make it so. Or does it?

In the tremulous world of the thing-in-itself, this is actually a cherry pitter—or stoner (no jokes, please). It's a clever device for removing the pits (or stones) from the fruit on a large scale, such as preparing freshly-picked cherries from a local orchard or backyard tree for canning. We had such a tree in the corner of our backyard and I have fond memories of the day each summer when we picked the cherries—my father and sisters and I up on ladders among the branches; my mother in the kitchen tending the bubbling pots and the battalion of waiting Mason jars. Except I never liked the dark-colored mass that later glopped out of the jars. I much preferred the artificial cherry flavoring of Kool-Aid or soda, a disappointment, no doubt, to my mother when she made pies. The dusty jars sat on basement shelves for more than twenty years, everyone afraid at that point to go near them.

Here the cherry pitter appears silvery but in fact it is cast iron, black as coal, its sheen a reflection of the lights. What to believe? The image is a reminder that, like a cherry, a photograph has at its core something that's hard to sink your teeth into. Namely, that a photograph isn't a window to the thing-in-itself. A photograph is its own thing-in-itself, with visions that can be very different than the thing portrayed. A photograph opens up a view into the emotions and associations of the viewer—a view *in* rather than a view *out*. If anything, it's more a mirror than a window. Though that may be unpleasant to accept if you can imagine the subject of this image crawling out from some dark corner. Headed your way.

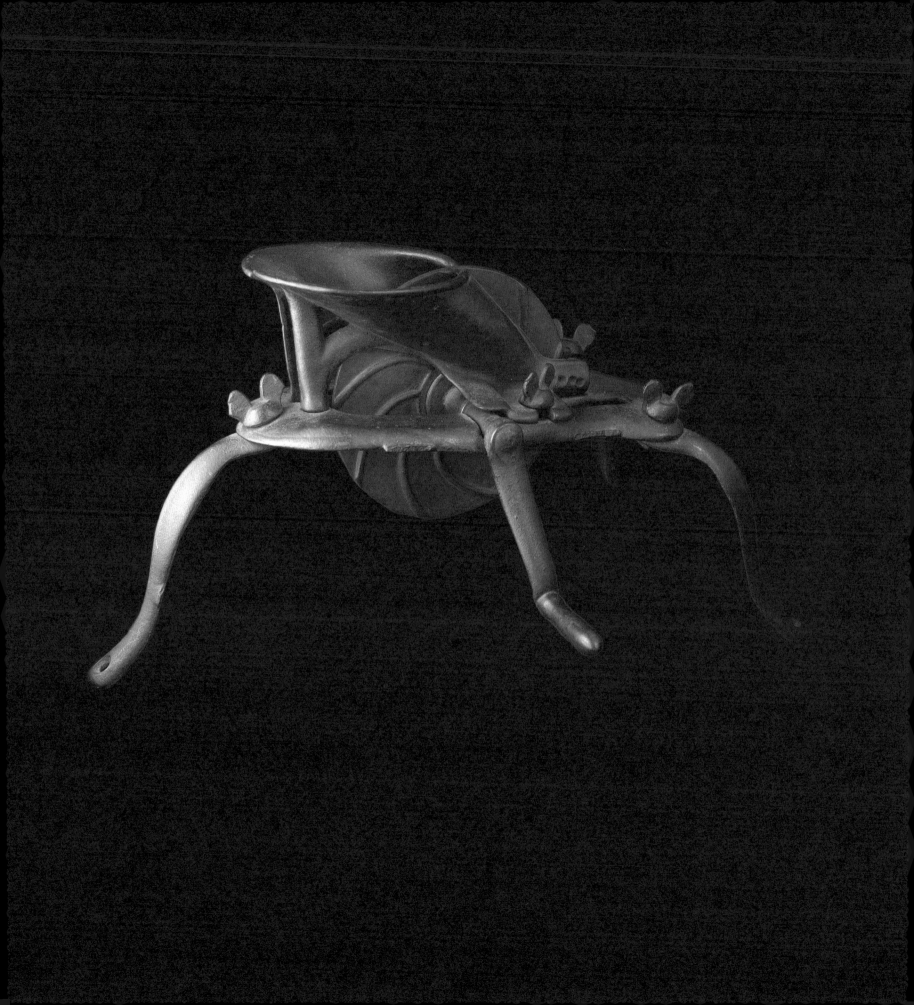

MASON JAR

A ways back in this narrative adventure, we talked about how the discovery of canning—the preservation of foodstuffs in metal cans—brought about the commercial food industry. In a similar way, the discovery of canning in Mason jars (a.k.a. fruit jars) brought preserving of foodstuffs home.

Before Mason jars, home canning required sealing wax, which was messy business at best; at worst, it was ineffective and therefore dangerous to one's health. Then in 1858, John L. Mason invented a machine that could cut threads inside a lid. That made it possible to manufacture glass jars with a rubber ring to create the seal and a screw-on lid to make sure it stayed that way. To commemorate the discovery, jars had "Patent Nov 30th 1858" embossed on the side. Home canning peaked between 1860 and 1900 and was popular not only with farmers and rural families, but also with urban families who started family traditions of "putting up" the results of their backyard gardens. Though a number of manufacturers made glass canning jars, the most aggressive, and the name most seen on the jars even today, was Ball.

If the jars weren't clear, they were usually in some shade of aqua—colored glass was thought to block light from reaching the food. The "Ball blue" jar seen here is sort of a hybrid. The lid features a bail closure or French Kilner, also known as a Lightning closure, first made by a number of manufacturers other than Ball, including the Atlas E-Z Seal. These jars were popular because no metal touched the food, eliminating the threat of rust, which could break the seal and contaminate the food; they were also easier to seal and remove, which is why they were called Lightning. This "Ideal" Ball jar bears the inscription "Pat D July 14 1908," but no clue as to why the date is marked.

Wikipedia and other sources tell us that Ball Mason jars achieved a different use during the Vietnam War. Chopper crews would pull the safety pin from a hand grenade and place the live grenade inside a jar to hold back the safety lever. During raids, the jars were easy to dump out the door; the grenades exploded when the jar shattered on impact, releasing the safety lever.

JAR LIFTER

In home canning, the lid with the rubber seal is placed on top of the jar, and the metal band screwed loosely over the lid to allow the steam to escape. Then the jar is placed in boiling water; when the jar is removed, the cooling creates a vacuum that seals the rubber gasket tight. This is true for both boiling water canning—used for acidic foods such as fruits, jams, apples, tomatoes—or pressure canning—used for low acidic foods such as beans, corn, carrots, meats. The utensil you see here is used to remove the jars from the hot water—

"Aren't you going to ask me?"

"Ask you what?"

"What I see. What this thingamajig reminds me of. It's a doozy."

"That's what I'm afraid of."

"I thought you wanted people to see these things as something else."

"I do. But first of all, I want them to see the things for what they are. For the thing-in-itself. They don't always have to remind people of something else. I'm hoping to portray them as interesting objects in and of themselves. If the image creates other associations, it just adds another layer or dimension of meaning and, hopefully, make it that much richer."

"Sounds complicated."

"Not really. It's like we see everything. I'm just trying to make you more aware of it."

Marty looks shifty. "I think you'd really like it. The thing I see."

"No, better keep it to yourself. I don't want to influence other viewers unnecessarily. . . ."

"It has to do with a barefoot Jack Lambert–type linebacker in a house dress. . . ."

"Saints preserve us!"

"Don't blame me. You're the one making these weird photos."

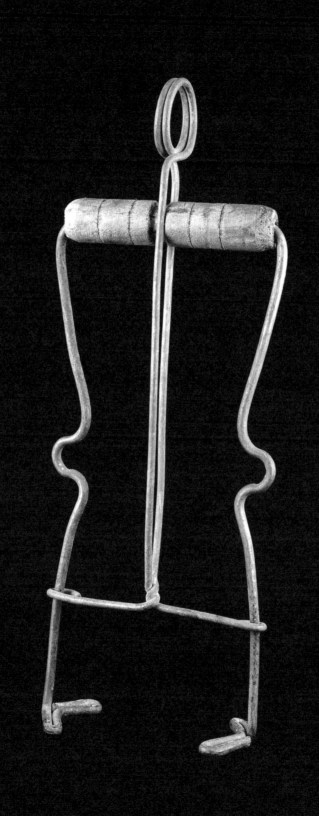

EGG BEATER

Form follows function. A touchstone of Modernism, it essentially means that the design of a thing should be determined by how it will be used. That might seem rather self-evident, but, as they say, there's no accounting for taste. In the cyclical nature of what's in and what's out, Post-Modernism turned the idea, if not inside-out, at least upside-down, so that designers could free their imaginations to include more whimsy, decoration, and downright fluff. All good things, of course—as you've undoubtedly noticed, I'm rather fond of whimsy myself. Still, when it comes to a basic kitchen utensil, it's probably a good idea to design a thing with an eye to its effectiveness.

Such as the egg beater that we see here.

The first egg beater was patented in 1856; since then, more than one thousand other egg beaters have been patented, and one hundred or so have been marketed, including the Archimedes (think a small, twisty pogo stick), the Ratchet, the Rope-Powered, the Water-Powered, and the Squeeze. But the basic handheld Rotary Beater has remained virtually unchanged since it was introduced by the Dover Stamping Company in 1869. Then as now, the design consists of wire or flat blades attached to two small cogged wheels, which in turn mesh with the cogs of a larger wheel turned by a handle. Traditionally, one turn of the handle results in five rotations of the blades. (Having read that in my research, I went down to the kitchen and tried it; darned if it's not true!) The Rotary Beater remains popular because it is easy to use and, due to the blades remaining in the liquid, little air is introduced into the mixture, giving the eggs a better texture. A case of the initial design holding up over the years. Form following function.

Collecting egg beaters is popular even with people who don't collect other kitchen things. My theory is that people love egg beaters because they are fun. Besides flicking the lever of an ice cream scoop, what's more fun in the kitchen than an egg beater? Leave an egg beater lying around and few people can resist picking it up and making those blades spin. Irresistible. *Whir-r-r-r!*

EGG SLICER

An egg slicer is a good example of the paradoxes that can come with efficiency. On one hand, there is the beauty of the thing's simplicity. Delicate as a fairy's harp; the precision of the ten strings fitting impeccably into ten awaiting slots; the provocatively-shaped cradle to hold the soft pale flesh of the egg. But then there is the moment of truth. *Schwick!* Something like a guillotine, only multiplied. What was an egg is no more. The roll-about oval shape is divided into perfectly proportioned, totally utilitarian slices. We don't know much about Humpty Dumpty's survival training, but even if he became hard-boiled to protect himself from a fall, Humpty without his shell would be no match for the cold efficacy of an egg slicer.

Angelic in appearance; a devil in its nature. A model of industrial design, form following function to the degree that it could seem like it's the other way around. In the annals of art photography, the egg slicer is something of a celebrity from an image by Edward Weston. But Weston's image was made with strong side-lighting to emphasize the geometric interplay of the slicer with its shadow, the character of the implement itself of no interest. In addition to eggs, the utensil can be applied to soft fruits and vegetables such as raspberries and mushrooms. It has even been used as a musical instrument, though the results, as you might expect, were rather tinkly.

What does an egg slicer have on its mind? The question might not be as loopy as it first sounds. A while ago, an article in *The New York Times Magazine* ruminated on the nature of consciousness. The idea was that consciousness, in order to form into complex systems such as our brains, must exist in every bit of matter, building up from some proto-level of existence beyond even photons and neutrinos and quarks. Granting that possibility, I can imagine our egg slicer thinking as it bites irreparably into the yielding flesh of the egg, *This is who I am.* As for the egg, I can hear a chorus of tiny interior voices—eleven, to be exact—if not exactly joyous, at least totally in the moment, all singing in concert, *Here we go!*

JELL-O MOLD

"It's all in the way you look at a thing. For instance, this Jell-O mold—I guess that's what it is. When you look at it straight on, it not only looks like a Jell-O mold—or whatever—it also looks like a Byzantine mosque, with all those pillars."

"I can see that," Marty says.

"But then, on the other hand, if you look at it slightly from below, as in this other picture, it looks like a space shuttle, rising into orbit.

"Yes, I can see that, too."

I smile kindly, the Knowledgeable Professor, instructing my enthralled student, proud of my sensitivity and perceptions. "Then again, if you turn it over and view it from the top as in this other picture, it looks like a hurricane from space—you'll notice the spiral is even counter-clockwise as they do in the Northern Hemisphere. That's the Coriolis force, caused by the rotation of the Earth and the inertia of the mass under the effect. But it only affects large bodies. You've heard that toilets spin clockwise in the Southern Hemisphere? Not true. . . ."

Marty hasn't been listening, thinking of something else. *Bad student, bad!*

"You see what I'm getting at, don't you?"

"Yes . . ." she says tentatively. I realize that I was too hard on her; she's just struggling with these concepts, is all. *Poor girl.* "I see what you're saying," she goes on, "except it doesn't seem that it's all in the way you look at it. It's more in the way you present it. If you didn't photograph it in these different positions, it would just look like a Jell-O mold."

She shrugs and gives a look that says, *So there, sorry.* It's hard to get good students these days.

CLIMAX MEAT GRINDER

A meat grinder named Climax. Cute. It's easy to imagine some early twentieth-century marketing managers having fun with that one—nudge, nudge; wink, wink. Okay, moving on. . . . When I was a child, this utensil was one of my first lessons in causality, the consequences of cause and effect. You cram the chunks of meat in here; you turn the crank; and the meat comes out there in a different form. In time, I came to understand the principle involved: The screw inside turned by the crank; the washer with the holes through which the meat was forced; the wing nut (like a small leaden angel) holding it all together. It wasn't scary exactly, but it certainly was something to consider. The seductive crank, just asking to be turned; the relentless whorls of the screw driving the meat to its transformation. Stick a finger in there and you'd learn the pain of causality fast.

Consequential thinking—the ability to foresee and grasp the consequences of one's actions—is not in everyone's makeup. For instance, my father had it, at least in some areas. An accountant with a cause-and-effect kind of mind, he could play several chess opponents at once—blindfolded; unfortunately, he tended to do the same with people. My mother, on the other hand, was more of an in-the-moment kind of gal. In regard to ground beef—this started with a meat grinder, remember—she was okay when she made her own, but the convenience products after World War II seemed to stymie her. When she bought ground beef at the A&P, she often let it sit in the grocery bags for a day or so before putting it in the freezer. Then when it came time to cook it, she plopped it frozen into a skillet of water and boiled it down to greasy gray mass. My brother saw it as malicious, but I think it more complicated than that. Regardless, such cooking explained why I grew up emptying a bottle of Heinz Ketchup every day.

You cram in the meat of reality here; you turn the crank of experience, geared to the screw of time; and out come memories there, ready to be patty-caked into sensibilities and dispositions. Of course, after all that, everything you think you know is anti-climactic.

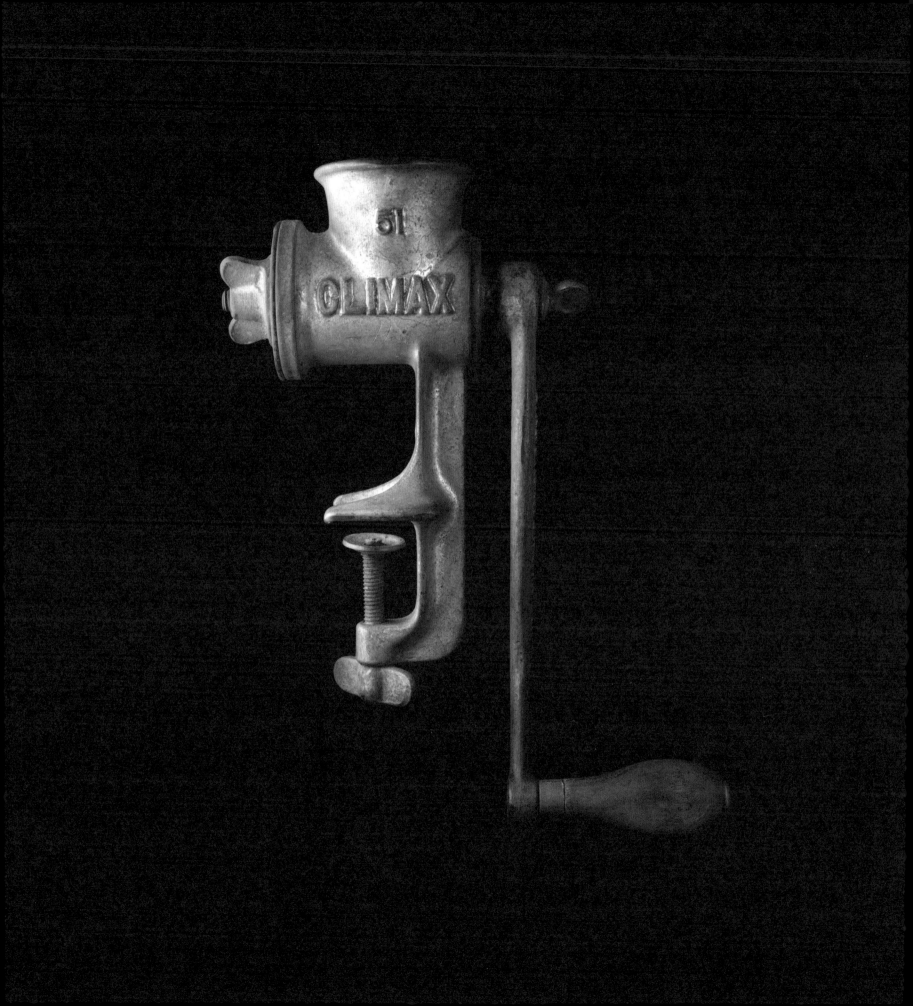

MEAT CLEAVER

The name Cleaver gained prominence in our collective consciousness during the mid-twentieth century from two totally opposite and in fact diametrically opposed sources. First, it was the name of the family on the most popular family TV show of the era, *Leave it to Beaver*, which chronicled a picture-perfect white suburban family, notable because it was the first such show written from the viewpoint of a child. It thereby either helped to establish or reflected upon the already-changing American culture that the child was, if not wiser, at least more aware than adults and, therefore, has the right to establish and arbitrate values. (Am I the only one to note that this precocious and [to me] unlikeable kid with the almost hot-looking mom was named Beaver Cleaver?) Additionally, Cleaver was the name of one of the era's most prominent African American activists and writers, Eldridge Cleaver, a founding member of the Black Panther Party whose avowed purpose was to at least redistribute—and at best burn down—everything that the Cleaver family had or dreamed of. But I digress.

A cleaver is the polite version of a butcher knife, a knife meant primarily for butchering and/or dressing animals. The butcher knife is said to play a key role in settling the American West in the late 1700s and early 1800s because it was the knife of choice for mountain men, those solitary trappers and hunters and guides who fled encroaching civilization only to find themselves inadvertently opening trails easily followed by those they were fleeing. A butcher knife was good for everything from skinning a beaver to scalping an enemy. Today, the heavier butcher knives are generally relegated to the meat-packing industry, whereas the cleaver finds a home in gentile households, taking its place in a matched display of cutlery hanging on a wall.

Incidentally, a cleaver doesn't need to be particularly sharp, because its cutting action is more from weight and pressure than movement to make its way through the molecular structure of bone. Too sharp and the blade will stick. Hard to withdraw for another cut. Another swing. Something a mountain man or a butcher needs to consider. Or a writer who makes cutting remarks.

BUTCHER KNIFE

Knives have been around for more than two-and-a-half million years, says Wikipedia, as witnessed by the Oldowan tools. In case you're not up on your archeology—I certainly wasn't—Oldowan tools refers to the Olduvai Gorge site in Tanzania where Louis Leakey found evidence of a stone tool industry. It's interesting to me that archeologists aren't sure which Hominines—humans, apes, or chimpanzees—actually made these tools, but the nod usually goes to an early human species. I also wonder why knives are referred to as the first tools—seems to me it would be a toss-up as to whether our early ancestors first made implements to cut or to pound. No matter.

Because of a blade's magical ability to separate another object into many—the physical manifestation of the mathematical principle of division—certain cultures through the ages have given knives spiritual and religious meaning. I know in our household, we use one paring knife with a serrated edge, particularly when it comes time to slice mushy things with a skin, such as tomatoes or freshly boiled red-skin potatoes.

Though most modern knives have either fixed or folding blades, kitchen knives, because they have no reason to hide their intention, are nearly always of the former persuasion. The number of types of knives in the kitchen are staggering: There are, in addition to paring knives, bread knives, boning knives, carving knives, chef's knives, electric knives, French knives, oyster knives, coring knives, table knives, steak knives, butter knives, fish filets, ham slicers, salmon slicers, tomato knives, bagel knives, utility knives, butcher knives, clam knives, vegetable knives, somitars, specialty knives, decorating knives, sandwich knives, mincing knives, cake knives, small bird knives, produce knives, citrus knives, salami knives, Panini knives, rabbit boning knives, poultry knives, cheese knives, sole knives. . . . And then there are all the Japanese sushi knives, which include gyutos, debas, usubas, nakiris, yanagis, sujihikis, katsuo hochos, sushikiris, takohi kis, sasakiri bochos—well, you get the idea.

If knives are the first tool, one would think a knife would also be the first murder weapon; though the Bible doesn't say, Cain probably wasn't in the tool business, being more of a pounder.

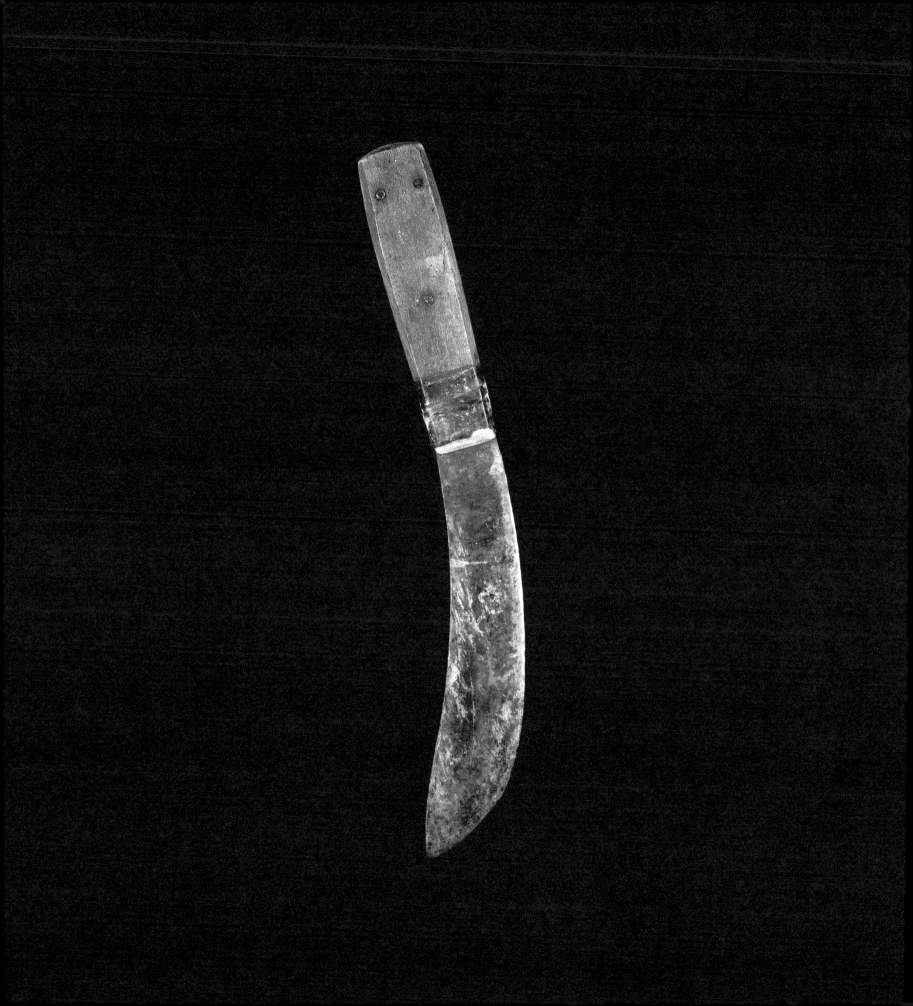

SILVER MEAT FORK

"Mary had a little lamb. . . ."

"Don't call me Mary."

"Your name is Mary Martha."

"It's Marty."

"And you had a little lamb. You said so."

"Sarah Agnes Josephine."

"Who?"

"That was the lamb's name. My dad used to say that whenever he was pissed; I think he liked the rhythm of it, like Jesus H. Christ. Sarah Agnes Josephine. But we called her Agnes."

"Was Agnes a 4H project?"

"No, my dad got her for us, me and my brother and sister. It was payment for something he did for one of the neighboring farmers, probably inseminating some cows. My dad drove us over and we kids were allowed to pick it out. She was the cutest little thing you ever saw. We all just loved her. We kept it down at Grandpap's barn. We'd go down every day or so and play with her."

"Did your grandpap have other sheep on the farm?"

"No, Agnes was the only one." Marty thinks a moment. "You remember how I told you that we always had Sunday dinner down at the farm? One Sunday we were there having dinner and Grandpap smacks his lips and says, 'You know, Agnes cooked up pretty good.'"

"They cooked Agnes?"

Marty nods. "Butchered her in the fall along with the hogs. That's why they kept her, but we kids didn't know; we thought she was our pet."

"That's terrible."

"That's life on a farm." Marty thinks a moment. "You know, I never did like lamb."

WHETSTONE

"How!"

"How what?"

"You've got me looking at these things differently. And that's what this sort of looks like to me, like an Indian holding up his palm to say hello. 'How!'"

"You know, of course, that Indians never went around saying 'How.' That's just some screenwriter's fantasy. A caricature of Indian language. Or worse."

"That's what Tonto always said on *The Lone Ranger*. 'How, kemo sabe.'"

"There's a theory that it actually means, 'Kill this oppressive White Man.'"

"That's not funny. So, what does it look like to you?"

"I think of it as a spear. A rather short spear admittedly. It's actually a knife sharpener."

"At least we agree it looks primitive. And sharpening knives seems rather primitive, when you think about it. Men sitting around a campfire, sharpening their knives for the hunt in the morning."

"Some knife sharpeners are sophisticated. Like this one."

"I'd say it looks like that instrument an eye doctor uses to examine your pupil. 'Look at my forehead, please.'"

"I guess I have only myself to blame." When Marty gives me a questioning look, I put on my best innocent smile. Marty doesn't buy it for a second.

"If that's a knife sharpener with those gears, I don't understand . . . you know . . . where the knife . . . I mean what you do with . . ."

"You mean how—"

"How!" Marty smiles and holds up an open palm. Her quarry having stepped in the trap.

KNIFE SHARPENER

Marty gives me a look that says, *You've got to be kidding me.*

"It's another kind of knife sharpener," I say.

Marty just shakes her head, as though I'm a hopeless case, and heads back downstairs.

"It's another kind of knife sharpener!" I call after her.

RICER

A potato ricer would appear to be an oxymoron, a device with the curious function of making one starchy foodstuff look like another. In fact, its name comes from the holes in the strainer plate that are about the size of grains of rice, though what squeezes out on the other side is more like mush than individual grains. The device is used most commonly to make mashed potatoes, though it can also be used to press excess water from sliced or grated potatoes. A potato ricer is also useful in *lefse* (a round Norwegian flatbread that resembles a tortilla made with mashed potatoes), *spätzle* (German noodles made of flour, milk, eggs and salt and squeezed through a ricer into boiling water), and homemade *gnocchi* (small Italian dumplings made from potatoes, semolina, and flour). It is also used for making *spaghettieis*—pronounced "spaghetti ice"—a German concoction where light-colored ice cream is squeezed through a press to make it look like a plate of spaghetti, topped off with strawberry sauce for tomato sauce and coconut flakes to represent parmesan cheese. Why you'd want to is another matter.

Enough potatoes are grown worldwide, they say, to cover the state of Rhode Island with potato plants. Though there are about five thousand varieties of potatoes, they all seem to have originated from Southern Peru, where they were domesticated as much as ten thousand years ago. After the Spanish conquered the Incas, who worshipped the potato, they introduced potatoes to Europe in the late 1500s. European farmers were slow to cultivate them, however, considering the tubers evil and causing among other things leprosy and uncontrolled sexuality. Speaking of which, Sir Walter Raleigh, well-known roué, introduced potatoes to Ireland, where they became an important food staple, as they eventually did throughout Europe, though the lack of genetic diversity left them vulnerable to disease and led to the Great Irish Famine in the middle of the nineteenth century. The result was more genetic diversity in the growing of potatoes, and more Irish diversity in the populating of America. As for Raleigh, he eventually lost his head, but it had nothing to do with potatoes.

THE
THINGS THEY
ATE

....

Part 2

CHUB'S RECIPE BOX

"Where did you get this recipe box?" I ask Chub, trying to ease her back into the subject of the recipes she used.

"It was one of those promotion things," she says, sitting across from me at her dining room table. "You know, you collect so many coupons or such-and-such, and send them in and they send you the box."

"I love the image of the Indian maiden, scanning the lake and the distant forest, as if searching for Sweet Cream Butter. Or maybe that's the translation of her Indian name; she's Princess Sweet Cream Butter."

Chub gives me the look she was famous for among second graders in the Fort Cherry School District. *Just settle yourself, young man.*

make a point at one end and with a grease pen write the name of the plant and the date planted. Works great. — Faye Ledward, Talent, Ore.

WINDOW CLEANER

Q. Some time ago in the paper you had a recipe for a window cleaner. I made a batch and found it was wonderful, no streaks or smears, but I put the article away and can't find it. I'd appreciate your printing it again in the paper. — Irene Repay, Whiting, Ind.

A. Here it is. Simply add ½ cup of vinegar to ½ gallon of water. Fill a spray container and it's ready to use. For a sparkly window, mist the window well, then dry with crumpled newspaper, an added recycling hint. I'm sending you a copy of my vinegar pamphlet. should send $2 and a self-

A Recipe From Chut 7/4/76
LIBBY WHITE

SWEET CREAM BUTTER

BAKED BEANS

This is a Depression-era recipe from when the woman known as Aunt Mary E—Chub's father's sister—did the cooking on the White Family Farm. When asked if this was a favorite dish, Chub says, "We ate baked beans because we had to, not because we wanted to." Interesting that a dish that was once necessary is now associated with fun times—warm days and family picnics and the Fourth of July.

Ingredients

2 lb. dried navy beans

1 med onion, sliced

1 tblsp salt

4 tsps cider vinegar

1 tsp prepared mustard

½ lb salt pork

2 qt cold water

½ c. molasses

2 tblsp brown sugar

$\frac{1}{16}$ tsp black pepper

hot water, if needed

Method

Pick over; wash beans thoroughly. Add cold water; cover, heat to boiling, simmer for 30 min. Drain; do not discard liquid. Place onion slices in bottom of bean pot. Combine next 7 ingredients; turn into bean pot. Add beans and enough hot drained liquid to cover (approximately 2 ½ c.). Arrange salt pork slices on top. Cover. Bake in very slow (250°) oven 7–8 hours.

After 4 hrs., remove 2 c. beans and mash. Then carefully stir into remaining beans. Cover, continue to bake. Add hot bean liquid or water as needed. Beans should be just covered with thick, luscious liquid.

Remove cover 1 hr. before end of cooking time and allow salt pork to brown.

Makes 10–12 servings.

BAKED BEANS   AUNT MARY E

2# DRIED NAVY BEANS   2qt COLD WATER
    1 MED ONION, SLICED
1 tblsp SALT   4 tsps CIDER VINEGAR   1/2 c MOLASSES
1 tsp PREPARED MUSTARD   2 tblsp BROWN SUGAR
1/4 c TOMATO KETCHUP   1/16 tsp BLACK PEPPER
    1/2# SALT PORK   HOT WATER, IF NEEDED

PICK OVER; WASH BEANS THOROUGHLY. ADD COLD WATER;
COVER, HEAT TO BOILING, SIMMER FOR 30 MIN. DRAIN; DO
NOT DISCARD LIQUID. PLACE ONION SLICES IN BOTTOM
OF BEAN POT. COMBINE NEXT 9 INGREDIENTS; TURN
INTO BEAN POT. ADD BEANS AND ENOUGH HOT DRAINED
LIQUID TO COVER (@ 2 1/2 c)

BAKED BEANS (2)
ARRANGE SALT PORK SLICES ON TOP. COVER. BAKE IN
VERY SLOW (250°) OVEN 1-8 HOURS. THEN
AFTER 4 HRS. REMOVE 2 c BEANS AND MASH. THEN
CAREFULLY STIR INTO REMAINING BEANS. COVER,
CONTINUE TO BAKE. ADD HOT BEAN LIQUID OR
WATER AS NEEDED. BEANS SHOULD BE JUST
COVERED WITH THICK, LUSCIOUS LIQUID.
    REMOVE COVER 1 HR BEFORE END OF COOKING TIME
ALLOW SALT PORK TO BROWN.
        10-12 SERVINGS

CORN MEAL MUSH

This recipe, from the Ultimate Farm Wife Aunt Helen, was a favorite of Chub's husband, Bill. I know this first hand because Marty keeps serving it to me, in the belief that if her father loved it, it stands to reason that I do too. Which I do, but still. As Chub notes, you make it ahead of time and have it on hand; it's usually a substitute for pancakes, but her family tended to have it at any meal.

"If you were Italian, you'd call it polenta," I say.

"We're Scotch-Irish," Chub says, "and it's mush."

Ingredients

8 cups water,   1 T salt
bring to boil   2–2¼ c. cornmeal

Method

Best flavor is from corn ground of kernel (not commercial variety). Add cornmeal slowly to boiling water (or moisten meal w/ cold water). The amount of cornmeal determines thickness of mush. Old saying, "Add meal until pudding sticks or wooden spoon doesn't fall over." Cook for ½ hr or more. Turn into cold water rinsed bread pan and chill.

Slice and dip in flour and fry in hot fat or lard. When both sides are golden brown, serve w/ butter, hot syrup, jam or honey.

Corn Meal Mush   Great Aunt Helen White

8 cups water   1 T salt
Bring to boil   2 - 2¼ c cornmeal

Best flavor is from corn ground of kernal (not
commercial variety) Add cornmeal slowly to boiling
water (or moisten meal w/cold water. The amount of
cornmeal determines thickness of mush. Old saying "add
meal until pudding sticks or wooden spoon doesn't
fall over." Cook for ½ # or more. Turn into cold
water rinsed bread pan and chill.
    Slice and dip in flour and fry in hot fat or
lard. When both sides are golden brown,
serve w/ butter, hot syrup, jam or honey.

HAM LOAF SUPREME

Though she liked ham, Chub generally wasn't fond of ham loaf—"It was always too salty. No matter what you did to it. Just a bit of persnickety me." Though she thinks this recipe might be okay—"The mixture of the pork with the ham would help to calm it down." I've noticed that Chub generally likes things calmed down.

Ingredients
1 lb. ground smoked ham
1 lb. ground lean pork
2 eggs
¾ c. round buttery cracker crumbs
¾ c. milk
salt to taste
pepper—optional

Method
Mix all ingredients and bake in loaf pan at 325°F until done (1½ –2 hrs).

   Yields – 6 servings

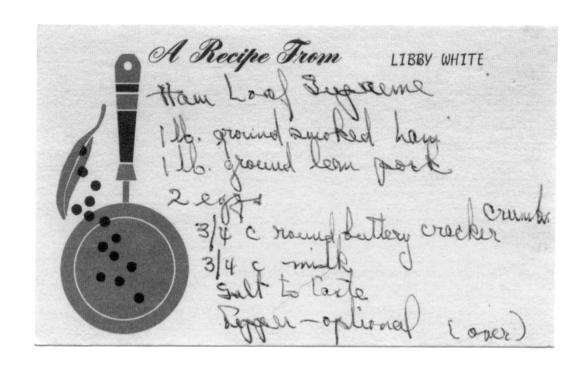

A Recipe From   LIBBY WHITE

Ham Loaf Supreme
1 lb. ground smoked ham
1 lb. ground lean pork
2 eggs
3/4 c round buttery cracker crumbs
3/4 c milk
Salt to taste
Pepper — optional   (over)

Mix all ingredients & bake in loaf pan
at 325°F. until done (1½ — 2 hrs.)
          Yield — 6 servings

INDIAN SUMMER BEEF STEW

Another recipe from the Ultimate Farm Wife, Aunt Helen. "You know what this is?" Chub says. "It's a garden gathering. This is farm-woman typical. Making do with whatever's on hand. You grab the last string beans off the vine, the last tomatoes, maybe even throw a leftover ear of corn in there. And you can't write down the quantities of anything because you don't know what you're actually going to use."

"So the result is like a ratatouille," I offer.

Chub shrugs. "If you say so."

Ingredients and Method

One pound or more of chunks of stewing beef dredged in seasoned flour. Brown in melted fat. Cover with water and cook for 1½ hours in covered saucepan (or until meat is tender). Add: 1 acorn squash, peeled and cut into squares. 2 cups green lima beans, 2 cups kidney beans (cooked or use 1 can), 1 onion cut up, 1 tsp. thyme, ¼ tsp. marjoram, (or use seasoned salt, add to meat). Put squash on top. Serve when vegetables are done.

Indian Summer Beef Stew

One pound or more of chunks of stewing beef dredged in seasoned Flour. Brown in melted fat. Cover with water and cook for 1½ hours in covered saucepan (or until meat is tender.) Add: 1 acorn squash, peeled and cut in squares. 2 cups green lima beans, 2 cups kidney beans (cooked or use 1 can), 1 onion cut up, 1 tsp. thyme, ¼ tsp marjoram, (or use seasoned salt, add to meat). Put squash on top. Serve when vegetables are done.

SALMON LOAF

Fresh fish was rare on the farm, unless somebody caught something in a stream; fresh seafood was unheard of. Chub says they occasionally had salmon loaf, but more often than not they just put the canned salmon on a plate on the table and had lemon to go with it. Fresh seafood, in a way. . . .

Ingredients
1 – 1-lb. tin salmon
1 – T lemon juice
1 – t salt – dash pepper
2 eggs, beaten
⅔ c. chopped celery
1⅓ c. bread crumbs
½ c. evaporated milk
½ c. liquid (fish juice and water)

Method
Bake 350°—30–40 min.

Mustard Sauce / Fish Sauce
1 c. milk
2 T. flour
Shake in jar.
After cooking add:
1 t celery salt
1 T prepared Mustard
⅛ t pepper

Salmon Loaf
1 - 1-lb tin salmon
1 - T lemon juice
1 - t salt - dash pepper
2 eggs beaten
2/3 C chopped celery
1½ C bread crumbs
½ t baking powder
½ C evaporated milk
½ C liquid (fish juice & water)
Bake 350° — 30-40 min.   over

Mustard Sauce   Fish Sauce
                                          after cooking
1 C milk)   add 1 t celery salt
2 T flour) shake in
              jar
Add
     1 T prepared Mustard
     1/8 t pepper

SCALLOPED OYSTERS

Marty tells me this was a great family favorite, eagerly anticipated at reunions and church suppers. When I mention to Chub that I never think of oysters as a Western Pennsylvania dish, she says, "Well, they're canned oysters," as if that explains it. She adds that she was never fond of oysters herself, something about the texture, or maybe just the idea of them. In typical home-spun fashion, the recipe never states how many oysters to use—your call.

Ingredients
4 T. Flour

4 T. Butter

2 c. "rich" milk

Method
Blend for white sauce and cook.

Add oysters to white sauce and "layer" with cracker crumbs, beginning and ending with cr. crumbs. Dot with butter on top.

Bake at 375°F for 20 min. or till "bubbly."

Here's what's cookin': *Scalloped Oysters*   Serves: _____

Recipe from the kitchen of: *Aunt Helen - Evelyn White*

4 T. Flour   2 c. "rich" milk

4 T. Butter   blend for white sauce

       and cook.

Add oysters to white sauce

and "layer" with cracker crumbs

beginning & ending with cr. crumbs.

Dot with butter on top.

Bake at 375° F. for 20 min. or till "bubbly."

GRAPE JELLY MEATBALLS

I make no bones about it: I tell Chub that I think this sounds atrocious. But she coos when she sees the recipe: "Oh these are delicious." This was another dish that one of her co workers brought for a teacher's luncheon and Chub told her she had to have the recipe. I ask if they're meant for kids, but she says, "No, they're for everyone. It's all in the way they're prepared." I say that's exactly what I'm afraid of. Chub looks at me sadly, as if to say there's just no accounting for taste. Or sons-in-law.

Ingredients
3 pkg armour frozen meatballs
(or make your own)
40 oz. jar ketchup
⅔ large jar grape jelly

Method
Place meatballs in pan. Cover with ketchup and jelly. Mix halfway through. Cook for 1½ to 2 hours—350°F.

Recipe for: _____ Emma Johnston

From the kitchen of: **Grape Jelly Meatballs**

_____

3 pkg armour frozen meatballs (or make your own)

40 oz jar ketchup

⅔ large jar grape jelly.

_____

Place meatballs in pan.

Cover with ketchup and jelly.

Mix half way through.

Cook for 1½ to 2 hours - 350°

_____

Makes: _____

1987 CURRENT INC COLORADO SPRINGS CO 809

SWEET NOODLES

These noodles live up to their name, with ingredients such as sugar, vanilla, and the juice from canned crushed pineapple—plus a topping of cinnamon and frosted flakes. Chub tells me they were a popular—and appreciated—item at a number of funeral dinners, particularly those of her own family. In the space of two years back in the 1970s, Chub lost her husband, teenage son, and pre-teen youngest daughter to congenital heart failure. When I asked her once how, after all that had happened, she was able to go on, she only smiled and said, "Because that's what we're here to do."

Ingredients
2 oz. melted margarine
½ lb. spring noodles, cooked and drained
2 eggs
1 c. milk
1 t vanilla
½ c. sugar
½ c. cottage cheese
1 c. sour cream
7 oz. crushed pineapple (not drained)

Topping
1 c. frosted flakes
1 T cinnamon
1 St.* oleo (melted)

Method
Bake 400°. 55–60 min.

---

* Stick

Sweet Noodles

2 oz. melted margarine

½# spring noodles cooked + drained

2 eggs

1 C milk

1 t vanilla

½ C sugar

½ C cottage cheese

1 c sour cream

7 oz crushed pineapple - (not drained)

Good - from Janet Michael

Topping

1 C frosted flakes

1 T cinnamon

1 St. oleo - (melted)

Bake 400°
55-60 min.

HELEN'S ONION CASSEROLE

Aunt Helen was French-Canadian; she and Clare met while they were both going to college in Michigan. She heard that Clare had a farm and thought he must be well-to-do. They got married and then she came here and, as Chub describes it, "found out he was not-so-well-to-do." But Helen stuck it out; she worked hard and had four children. She was the all-around farm wife—as Chub notes, "She would have made a good executive secretary, too; she was good at delegating things."

"In other words," I say, "she could be bossy."

Chub shrugs. "That's certainly one word for it."

Ingredients
8 medium onions
¼ c. butter
½ c. rice
salt and pepper*

Method
Slice† thin, melt butter.

    Add onions‡ and stir to coat.

    Boil 5 min. and drain.

    Add§ to onions, cover and bake in 350° oven for about an hr. 15 min. before serving. Add 2–4 T. cream and sprinkle ¼ c. grated cheese.

---

*   You will also need 2–4 tablespoons of cream and ¼ c. grated cheese.

†   Slice onions

‡   to butter

§   Rice, salt, and pepper

Helen's casserole

8 med onion ⎫ Slice thin melt butter
¼ c. butter ⎬ add onions & stir
            ⎭ to coat.
½ c. rice — Boil 5 min & drain
    Salt & Pepper
Add to onions, cover & bake in
350° oven for about an hr. 15
min before serving add 2-4 T.
cream & sprinkle ¼ c. grated cheese

CARROT PUDDING

This is Chub's famous Carrot Pudding recipe, which is actually more of a soufflé than a pudding. "You can turn up your nose if you care to," she says, noting my reaction to the name, "but it's a great way to introduce vegetables to kids. It tastes just like pumpkin pie." Darned if it doesn't.

Ingredients

2 c. carrots – cooked, cut in 1" pieces

3 eggs (low chol. – 4 egg whites)

1 tbsp. baking powder

2 tbsp. flour

1 c. milk (skim)

⅓ to ½ c. sugar

1 stick margarine

¼ tsp. cinnamon

Method

In blender*, mix **all** ingredients, blend (20–30 seconds).

Pour into baking dish (buttered) – bake at 350°F for 30 minutes or until silver knife inserted in center comes out clean.

---

* I usually put stick of margarine in saucepan with drained, hot carrots to melt some before mixing.

Carrot Pudding

2 c. carrots - cooked, cut in 1" pieces.

3 eggs   (low chol. - 4 egg whites)

1 tbsp. baking powder   ⅓ to ½ c. sugar

2 tbsp. flour   1 stick margarine

1 c. milk (skim)   ¼ tsp. cinnamon

In blender, mix *all* ingredients, blend (20-30 sec)

Pour into baking dish (buttered) - bake at
350° F. for 30 minutes or until silver
knife inserted in center comes out clean.

* I usually put stick of margarine in saucepan
with drained, hot carrots to melt some before
mixing.

52

5 CUPS SALAD

"I used to make this a lot. I didn't always use the coconut, but I liked the salad it made. I made this salad for the family, rather than to take somewhere—everyone I knew made a salad like this at home so there was nothing special about it, and if you're going to take a dish to the church or some place you want it to be special. You can use cans instead of cups, that's easier. And always use the small marshmallows—if you don't have the small ones, you can try to use the big ones but that always gets complicated; they get all sticky on your scissors and you end up with a terrible mess."

Ingredients
1 c. mandarin oranges
1 c. pineapple cubes
1 c. coconut
1 c. small marshmallows
1 c. sour cream

Makes 8–10 servings.

5 Cups Salad.

1 C Mandarin Oranges
1 C. Pineapple cubes
1 C. cocoanut
1 C Small Marshmallows
1 C Sour Cream

8-10 servings

RAW TOMATO RELISH

Aunt Ruth—Marty's aunt; Chub's younger sister—was known for a number of things in Hickory. She was a physical education teacher at the junior and senior high school for many years. She was one of the area's best farmers, running the family farm after her father died. There were her duets with Chub at their Presbyterian Church—Ruth's perfect pitch alto blending effortlessly with Chub's soprano—even though Ruth was legally deaf. (I have no idea how she managed that.) She was known for the variety of pickles and such that she canned each year. But it was her Raw Tomato Relish that brought out the most compliments. Incidentally, by including the option of hot peppers, she was only being polite. She actually considered such spicy food as being close to un-American.

Ingredients

1 peck* tomatoes

6 lb. green peppers

5 lb. onions

10 sm. hot peppers (optional)

1 c. salt

2 c. sugar

4 t white mustard seed

1 qt. vinegar

Method

Peel tomatoes and onions; remove seeds from peppers; chop using medium blade; add salt; place in jelly bag and drain for 24 hours. Remove from bag and add remaining ingredients. Mix well; place in clean jars and seal.

---

*   About 8 dry quarts

Here's what's cookin' Raw Tomato Relish Makes 4 qts.

Recipe from the kitchen of Aunt Ruth White

1 peck ripe tomatoes	1 c salt
6 lg green peppers	2 c sugar
5 lg onions	4 t celery seed
10 sm hot peppers	4 t white mustard seed
(optional)	1 qt vinegar

Peel tomatoes & onions; remove seeds from peppers. Chop using med. blade; add salt; place in jelly bag & drain for 24 hrs. Remove from bag & add remaining ingredients. Mix well; place in clean jars & seal.

BUTTERSCOTCH COOKIES

"Oh yes, Aunt Mary E's cookies," Chub says. "Good cookies but you end up with a mountain of them. She doesn't say here, but I think it's something like six or seven dozen—and they quickly turn into dipping cookies. I mean hard, you can break a tooth on them. But they are good cookies."

Ingredients
   2* | 4 cups sugar (2 white – 2 brown)
   3 | 6 cups flour
   1 | 2 tsp. soda†
   1 | 2 tsp. cream of tartar
   2 | 4 eggs (add pinch of salt)
   ½ | 1 cup lard and butter (half of each)
   1 | 2 tsp. vanilla
   ½ | A cup of nuts or raisins may be added if you wish.

Method
Work bumps out of sugar. Sift flour, soda, cream of tartar together and mix with sugar.

   Work in shortening. Add eggs last (beat eggs without separating until foamy). Put vanilla into eggs and add to first ingredients. Work until you can form into a roll or rolls. (Do not add any more flour.) Make rolls about two inches thick.

   Let stand overnight. Slice about ½ inch into thickness in morning and bake.

   Wishing you good luck.

---

*   Use the numbers on the left side of this line to halve the recipe for a smaller batch.
†   Baking soda

Butter - Scotch Cookies

2|4 cups sugar (2 white - 2 brown)
3|6 cups flour
1|2 tsp. Soda
1|2 tsp. Cream of Tartar
2|4 eggs (add pinch of salt)
½|1 cup lard and butter (half of each)
1|2 tsp. Vanilla
A cup of nuts or raisins may be added if you wish.

Work lumps out of sugar - Sift flour, Soda, Cream of Tartar together and Mix with sugar.
   Work in shortening — Add eggs last (beat eggs without separating until foamy) put vanilla into eggs and add to first ingredients. Work until you can form into a roll or rolls — (Do not add any more flour) — Make rolls about two inches thick.
   Let stand over night. Slice about ½ inch in thickness in morning and bake.
   Wishing you good luck.

Mary E White

GOBS*

"Yum-m-m-m-m," says Chub, looking at this recipe. "A good sticky cookie." It's also an assembly cookie: first you make the cookies, then you add the filling. "A different animal than an Oreo." Chub used to assemble a dozen or so of the gobs, then keep the rest of the cookies in a separate jar to keep them fresh. "A sticky cookie is one thing, but nobody likes a soggy gob."

Ingredients

Cream:
2 c. sugar
½ c. shortening
2 eggs

Sift and add dry ingredients, alternating w/liquid.
1 c. buttermilk
1 t vanilla
¾ c. boiling water
4 c. flour
2 t soda†
½ t baking powder
1 t salt
½ c. cocoa

Method

Bake on ungreased cookie sheet; 450° for 5 min.; cool and fill.
    Filling: 1 c. milk, 1 pkg vanilla instant pudding
    Whip: 1 c. shortening, 1 c. powdered sugar, 1 t. vanilla
    Make pudding; whip other ingredients; whip together until smooth.

---

* This is a double batch! Do **not** double again!!
† Baking soda

THIS IS A DOUBLE BATCH! DO NOT DOUBLE AGAIN!!

Here's what's cookin' GOBS   Serves

Recipe from the kitchen of GRANDMA BEARD

CREAM: 2 c SUGAR   1/2 c SHORTENING   2 EGGS

SIFT & ADD DRY INGREDIENTS, ALTERNATING W/ LIQUID.

1 c BUTTERMILK	4 c FLOUR
1 t VANILLA	2 t SODA
3/4 c BOILING WATER	1/2 t BAKING POWDER
	1 t SALT 1/2 c COCOA

BAKE ON UNGREASED COOKIE SHEET, 450° for 5 MIN, Cool & Fill.

Filling: 1 c MILK   1 pkg vanilla instant pudding

WHIP: 1 c shortening   1 c powdered sugar   1 t. vanilla

Make pudding; whip other ingredients; whip together until smooth.

SHOO-FLY PIE

The name is self-evident, if you think about it: This pie made with molasses is supposedly so sweet that it attracts flies. A dubious recommendation it seems to me, but Aunt Ruth, Chub's younger sister, had a taste for it. Ruth got this recipe from a friend in Mennonite country. The problem is that there is molasses, and then there is molasses—the taste can go from sugary to downright bitter. As for Chub, she never had a taste for molasses of any kind, light or dark, and when she first saw this recipe, said, "I don't believe I want any, thank you." But maybe it was just a sister thing.

Ingredients

Bottom Part:
¾ c. dark molasses
½ t soda*
¾ c. boiling water

Top Part:
1½ c. flour
¼ c. shortening
½ c. brown sugar

Method

Dissolve soda in hot water; add molasses. Combine sugar and flour; rub in shortening to make crumbs. Pour ⅓ liquid into an unbaked crust. Add ⅓ of crumb mixture. Alternate layers w/ crumbs on top.

Bake at 375° for approximately 35 minutes.

Makes 1 9-in. pie.

---

* Baking soda

PIES   SHOO-FLY   AUNT RUTH WHITE

BOTTOM PART:
   3/4 c DARK MOLASSES   3/4 c BOILING WATER
   1/2 t SODA

TOP PART:
   1 1/2 c FLOUR   1/2 c BROWN SUGAR
   1/4 c SHORTENING
          MAKES 1 9-in PIE
_____

Dissolve soda in hot water; add molasses. Combine
sugar & flour; rub in shortening to make crumps.
Pour 1/3 liquid into an unbaked crust. Add 1/3 of
crumb mixture. Alternate layers w/ crumbs on top.
   Bake @ 375° for @ 35 minutes.

"I was thinking about what you said about Aunt Libby never having the chance to become a good cook," I say, when it appears that Chub is through talking about recipes. "The thing about Marty is, she's absolutely fearless in the kitchen. She'll try all sorts of unusual combinations or proportions of ingredients, and nine times out of ten, it's terrific."

"Well, she didn't get that from me," Chub says. "I was always afraid to experiment like that."

"But you're a great baker; everybody says that."

"Baking was different. I always seemed to know intuitively what to do—when to add more butter or flour, what the proportions should be. But cooking was different. With baking, no one was waiting for the results, if something came out a tangled mess you had the chance to do it over. But with a meal, there were no second chances. People—people you loved—were waiting for what you made them. You didn't want to disappoint them."

She closes the lid, smiling at the image of the little Indian princess who scans her wilderness of forests and lakes, touches the box with a kind of reverence. No, it's more than that: thankfulness.

LAND O'LAKES

SWEET CREAM BUTTER

THE
THINGS THEY
USED

Part 3

NOODLE CUTTER

If asked the proverbial question of what I would like for my Last Meal, I know what it would be: lasagna. Why this white, Scots-Irish, Son-of-a-Certified-Public-Accountant should have such a fondness for Italian tomato-sauce-pasta-dishes in general, and lasagna in particular, undoubtedly has much to do with the universal appeal of tomato sauces and pasta. The odds were certainly against it in my case; my introduction to the genre was through canned spaghetti that my mother dished up at lunchtimes. Luckily, I eventually graduated to the real thing through the family of the Italian girl I almost married out of high school. During my college years and for the years before marriage (and between), I existed on a diet mainly of pasta and zucchini or spinach in marina sauce. Loved it.

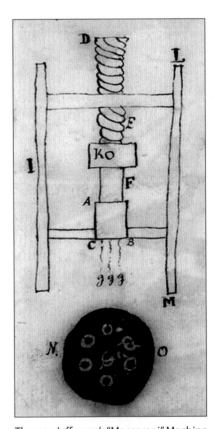

Thomas Jefferson's "Maccaroni" Machine

Pasta has been around forever, so to speak. More than three thousand years ago, Etruscans used tools that look like pasta dies and extruders and baked a dish made from wheat and egg paste; Ancient Greeks and Romans had a form of lasagna; in the fifth century the Talmud refers to cooking noodles. China, Japan, and India all had early dishes, probably long before they were known in the West. Italian and Spanish explorers carried pasta to the New World; Thomas Jefferson loved "maccaroni" so much, he designed his own machine to extrude it. Mac and cheese was popular during the time of the Civil War, though it was the large Italian immigration around the turn of the nineteenth century that brought widespread popularity of spaghetti, lasagna, and assorted friends.

Of course, then there's the question of what, exactly, is pasta. We know it's made from wheat and water, though Italian law says it can only be durum wheat flour or wheat semolina. But what if it's baked instead of boiled? Made from Spinach? The difference between pasta and noodles . . . ?

ALUMINUM POT

Okay, so what *is* the difference between pasta and noodles? I'm beginning to think nobody really knows for sure—and the definitions or usage change from country to country. In the United States, a noodle is pasta, but pasta isn't necessarily a noodle. We saw earlier that pasta is essentially semolina flour and water; if you add egg solids or yolk, you're in noodle country. As for all the shapes and sizes of pasta, they provide varying amounts of surface area for the different sauces to cling. For instance, compliments of Wikipedia . . .

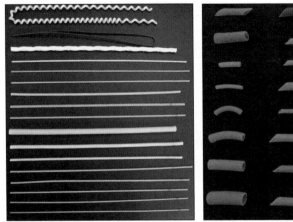

you have your long pasta . . .   and your short pasta . . .

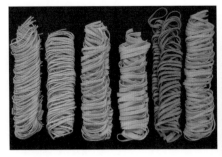

your fresh pasta . . .

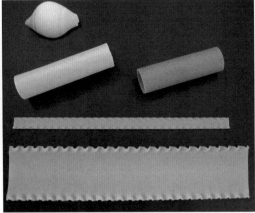

and your pasta for baking . . .

and dozens, maybe hundreds, of other varieties for cooks to noodle around with.

FOLEY FOOD MILL

A Foley Food Mill. An interesting if innocuous-looking fellow—after taking the image, it occurred to me that this guy had been through a lot—a kind of three-in-one utensil, a masher, ricer, and strainer, touted for making applesauce, mashed potatoes, separating the seeds from tomatoes, etc. You'd never know, just by looking at it, that it and its fellows stand accused of being unwitting accomplices in a plot to change the very nature of Mother-As-Nurturer.

The idea is put forth in an essay by Amy B. Werbel, reprinted in a book titled *American Artifacts*. According to Werbel, until the 1930s, child-rearing was based on a mother's own experience and expertise, including what children ate. In the late '20s and early '30s, however, there was a movement against Mother Knows Best; mothers were told they should listen to the professional advice of doctors and scientists (who, incidentally, were usually men). Spearheading this idea were ads for Gerber's Baby Food, Sunshine Biscuits, Cream of Wheat, Evaporated Milk, among others, as well as the child-rearing books and women's magazines of the day. A particular goal was to convince mothers to stop nursing their children as early as eight months and feed them prepared foods such as strained vegetables. To its credit, the Food Mill promoted straining the vegetables yourself—Mom could at least be trusted to do that. But advertisers countered by saying that prepared foods were safer because they prevented germs from getting into food. (*Oh, really!*) More than that, they hinted strongly that if a mother didn't feed her children prepared foods, she ran the risk of causing the child's vulnerability to disease, stunted growth, unattractive features, and even death. Mother-As-Nurturer became Mother-as-Self-Conscious Consumer. Sad.

Later generations—aided by some good investigative reporting—came to doubt the inherent safety of prepared foods, at the same time as (and maybe because of) the home-grown and fresh-from-the-farm movements have gained prominence. Ironically, as a low-tech utensil somewhere between a sieve and an electric blender, perhaps the time has come again for the Foley Food Mill.

GLASS BUTTER CHURN

"Benjamin Franklin's Bell Jar."

"What?"

"That's what this reminds me of. Didn't Franklin use a bell jar to capture lightning?"

"It's a butter churn. I'd think you'd know that."

"How would I know a butter churn from Ben Franklin's Bell Jar?"

"You're a farm girl."

"Well, first of all, I'm not really a farm girl. My parents lived next door to my grandparents, my mom's parents, who had a farm—and the Shantee Restaurant. It wasn't my parents' farm."

"No, but you used to be around it every day. You grew up around it."

"True. But I have to tell you I never really liked it all that much. I mean it was nice enough, but the cows, they scared me. And there were bugs . . . really big bugs." Marty shudders.

"So, I'm guessing you don't have any really good making-butter stories."

"None at all. Grandpap never made butter, as far as I know. And after he died it wasn't even a dairy farm anymore. My Aunt Ruth grew corn and wheat. I'm not even sure how butter is made."

"When you stir cream, the membranes that surround the milk fat dissipate and clumps form called butter grains. All this stirring stirs up air bubbles, and the butter grains attract other butter grains that clump together into fat globules, and eventually you get buttermilk. If you keep stirring long enough, the fat globules solidify and you drain off the buttermilk and you get butter. Incidentally, it's pretty sad when the guy born and raised in a steel town knows more about butter-making than the ersatz farm girl."

"Ersatz?"

"There's nothing wrong with that. It means—"

"I know what it means," Marty says, measured. And I wonder what *I've* stirred up.

BUTTER PADDLE

"That's just what I mean. What is that?"

"It's a butter paddle. It's to scrape the butter from the side of churn. . . ."

Marty looks like she just won something. "Exactly. But look at the way you chose to photograph it. Usually you take things head-on, but this time it's from the side."

"I tried it head-on, but you didn't get the sense of the curve. I thought—"

"But you knew this way it would suggest something else."

"Well, I—"

"You intentionally made it look like . . . well, I don't know what it looks like. A Shmoo."

"A Shmoo?"

"One of those funny little bottom-heavy creatures from *Li'l Abner*. . . ."

"You're showing your age."

"My mother told me about them. Or it's some phallic-thing or something. I don't know. I only know it doesn't look like what it is."

"Would you say it looks like *more* than what it is?"

"More. Other. Whatever. My point is that you're leading the interpretation of what it looks like."

"Of course. I'm the one taking the photograph."

"So it's as much you as it is the object."

"I never said otherwise. The photographer is the one doing the initial observation, if you will. What the photograph gives us is a record of that slice of the photographer's consciousness. The photographer influences the perception of the object, you might say, just like the act of perception through a consciousness influences the object itself."

Marty's eyes are beginning to glaze over. "There *is* a nice curve to it, isn't there?"

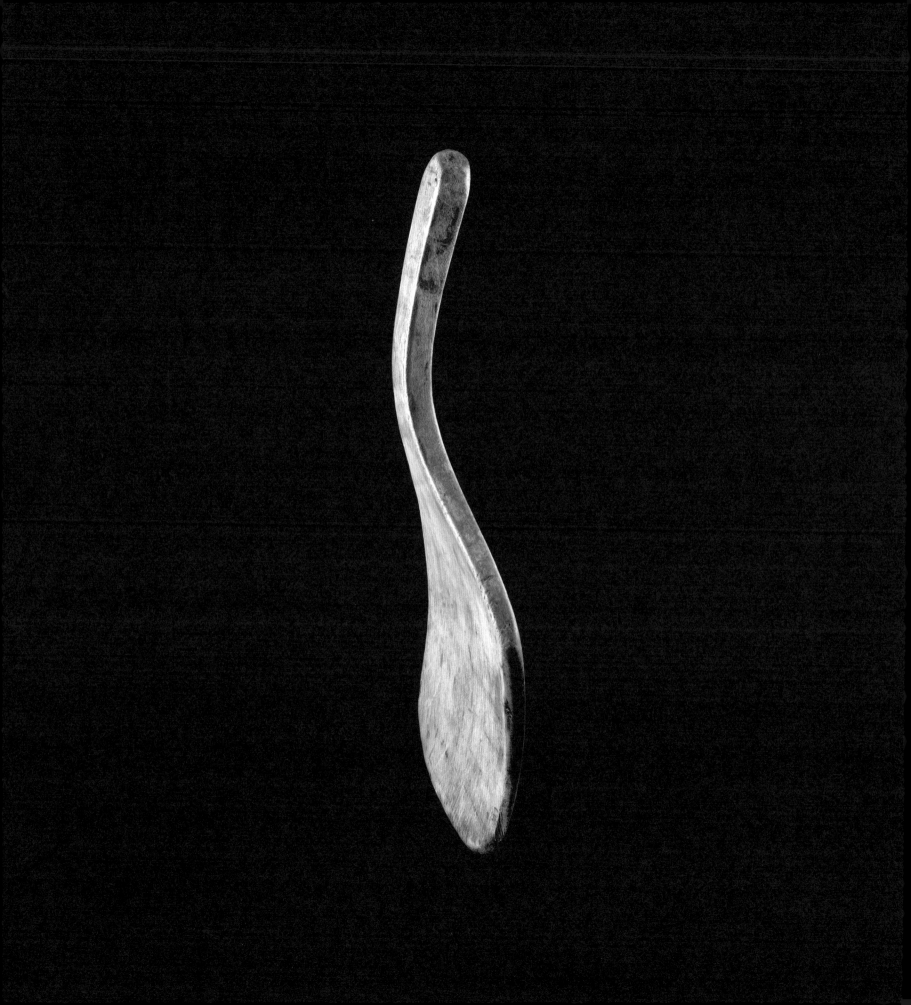

GLASS MIXER

Egg beaters were so popular—and quickly became an indispensable item in American kitchens—that they spawned countless imitators and innovators. One idea was to mount the apparatus on the wall or clamp it to a table so you didn't have to hold the thing while you whirred away. However, that meant you had to hold the bowl in which you were whirring, so the next idea was to attach a bowl or glass jar. Then it became a free-standing apparatus, with a crank on top with perforations rather than gears to drive the wheel and wire whips instead of beaters. The result was the New Keystone Beater, described in an 1885 patent as "a culinary beater or whipper the arms of which are expanded outward and held in their expanded positions by centrifugal force, whereby the said beater or whipper is enlarged in its diametric length. . . ." That sounded good, but the centrifugal force necessary to splay the whips would have been enough to send the device airborne. In practice, the whips stayed in their original configuration, though they tended to wobble around in their spinning, which actually helped the mixing process in the further reaches of the container.

These innovations, which influenced the development of the electric mixer—not to be confused with a blender, which is a different kind of animal: blenders have sharp blades and usually operate at higher speeds to chop, liquefy, and . . . well, blend—came from the North Brothers Manufacturing Company of Philadelphia, which produced a broad assortment of kitchen things, including such favorites as the Gem Ice Shave and the Lightning Ice Chipper. The North brothers were the epitome of early American entrepreneurs and perfect compliments to each other, Sheldon described as "a mechanical genius" and Ralph as "a bank-trained management man." Seems they were prescient, too, evidently figuring if folks were too lazy to whip eggs by hand, they would soon get tired of cranking. Despite the beater's early success, the brothers concentrated on their line of Yankee brand spiral screwdrivers, leaving another company to make the later models, such as the Even Full pictured here. Sure enough, in 1919, KitchenAid marketed the first home electric mixer.

JUICE KING

The Juice-King waves to his people! Long live the Juice-King!

Squeezing oranges and lemons and limes for their juice has been a popular pastime since citrus fruit originated in Southeast Asia. Almost as popular, it seems, as thinking up devices to do the squeezing. There are juicers, citrus juicers, fruit juice extractors, lemon squeezers, and reamers, to list a few, with names such as Ex-Squeeze-It, Handy-Andy, and the Juicy Salif, variously made of cast iron, glass, aluminum, ceramic, wood, and plastic. As a further reflection of that spate of ingenuity that brought about the industrialization of America, most of the more than two hundred patents held by the US Patents and Trademark Office were issued between 1880 and 1910.

The premise is simple enough: extract the juice without the pulp and seeds. But it's not as simple as it sounds. For instance, with electric juicers—which look like but shouldn't be confused with blenders—there are centrifugal, centrifugal ejection, masticating, manual press, single auger, dual cage auger, and twin press. *Whew!* Among squeezers, there are those where you turn the device while holding the fruit and those where you hold the device while the orange or lemon turns. The Juice-King shown here featured a patented lever mechanism and a long handle to gain leverage.

All this for a little juice. But the *Ladies Home Journal* seemed to squash it all way back in September 1889: "An old-time Philadelphia Housewife said yesterday: 'None of your new-fangled lemon squeezers for me. Anything, especially acid—squeezed through metal, such as many of the improved ones are, is very bad. The wooden ones do not have this fault: neither do those made of glass or porcelain. But they all have one fault that there is no getting rid of, and that is that the skin of the lemon is squeezed so that its flavor mixes with that of the juice. This is all wrong. There is but one way to squeeze a lemon, and that is the simple old-fashioned way, between your fingers. Plenty of power can be brought to bear, particularly if the lemon is well-rolled first.'"

The Juice-King is dead! Long Live the Juice-King!

FRUIT REAMER

One is tempted to think that all these squashing and squeezing devices—such as the scepter- or jet-engine-like Reamer pictured here—is a bit of overkill just to get some juice from an orange or lemon. Matter of fact, most people skip the problem altogether: approximately two-thirds of Americans drink store-bought orange juice. But that raises some curious paradoxes. . . .

The most popular brand of orange juice—in the United States as well as Latin America, Europe, and Central Asia—makes much of the phrase "not from concentrate," suggesting its pasteurized juice is fresher and better than those made "from concentrate" and therefore worth a higher price. Fact is, storing full-strength orange juice is a costly business, involving a process called deaeration that strips the juice of its oxygen so it won't oxidize in the million-gallon storage tanks where it can be kept for up to a year. But that's not the funny part; the funny part is that when you strip the oxygen, you also strip the flavor-providing chemicals. So, juice companies hire flavor and fragrance companies, the same ones that devise perfumes for Dior and Calvin Klein, to design "flavor packs" to put back in the juice to make it taste fresh. Flavor packs, incidentally, that aren't listed in the ingredients; technically, they are derived from orange essence and oil, but, as one writer notes, "resemble nothing found in nature." Americans, it seems, like juice with a fragrance high in ethyl butyrate, whereas Mexicans and Brazilians favor packs with *decanals* or terpene compounds.

"So even though it's more or less derived from oranges," Marty puts in, "you could say there's something imitation about it as well."

What's she getting at? Shields up, Mr. Sulu, Red alert! "Yes, I suppose you could say. . ."

"So you could say it's sort of ersatz orange juice."

"Yes, I guess you could . . . sort of . . ."

Marty gives her secret smile and hums to herself as she moves away. Like she knows something that I'm going to wish I did.

FAMILY SCALE

"Who's this Columbia Family," Marty says, "and how did you get their scale?"

Take it easy. She's only making a joke, she doesn't mean anything by it. Why are you always so suspicious?

"Probably named for the Columbia Exposition in 1893," I tell her. "A lot of things were."

"So, what did a 'family' weigh on it?"

She's just curious, that's all, she doesn't mean anything by it. "Babies, most likely."

"As long as they didn't weigh over twenty-four pounds," Marty says wryly. "And had good balance."

Through the first half of the twentieth century, the Landers, Frary & Clark Company was one of the best-known and prestigious manufacturers of housewares and hardware, making everything from steel bull-nose rings to electric ranges. In the 1890s, it introduced a series of revolutionary household products under the Universal name: the Universal bread maker that prepared bread dough to rise overnight; the Universal Food Chopper that turned anything it touched into hash; and the Universal Coffee Percolator that brewed coffee below the boiling point of water to improve flavor. At one time, six out of every homes in the United States had at least one Universal product. Their Columbia household scale was touted to be "the first product designed particularly for the American Housewife."

Scales

No. 249—The Columbia Family Scale. A slanting dial family scale weighing by the ounce up to twenty-four pounds. These scales are made of sheet steel and are finished in black enamel, and have white enameled dial. They take up but little space, are accurate and reliable. The scale top is square and flat in order to readily place all kinds of articles on it, and the scale may be regulated by a brass screw projecting through top of balance box. Made by Landers, Frary & Clark, New Britain, Conn.

Columbia Scale

"I know what you're thinking," I say, "it's only an ersatz scale, right?"

She looks at me as if trying to ignore a string of mucous dangling from my nose. "No, I wasn't thinking that at all. Maybe you need to, hmm, *weigh* your comments more carefully."

Her eyes twinkle and I think, *Oh, she's good. She's really good. I don't stand a chance.*

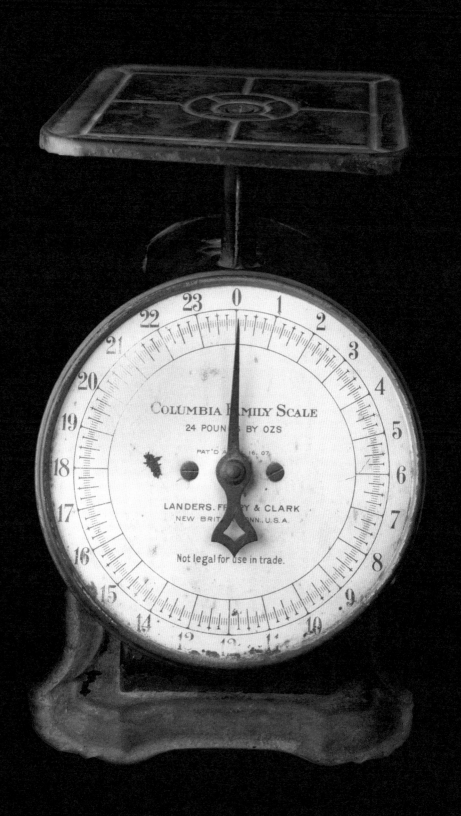

SOAP SAVER

Soap is a pretty important kitchen thing, if you think about it, unless you have a particular fondness for ptomaine and other food poisonings. The Second Law of Thermodynamics says that everything falls into disorder or entropy over time, which means, in a practical application, that the kitchen that starts out sparkling clean in the morning will fall into chaos and germs by the time you're done working in it at the end of the day. Which is where soap comes in.

As Tyler Durden says in the movie *Fight Club*, soap is the yardstick of civilization. Recipes for soap— basically a chemical reaction between a weak fatty acid and a strong alkali—go back as far as the Babylonians in 2800 BC. Ancient Greeks used a mixture of lye and ashes to clean pots; Romans used soap for cleaning clothes, though it's an early urban legend that it was named for Mount Sapo and was discovered by washerwomen along the Tiber who made use of the animal fat that ran off the altars and mixed with the ashes of the sacrificial fires. Soap for personal cleansing was used in Western civilization by the third century AD, but declined during the Dark Ages until it came back into fashion in the 1600s. Soap making in America was pretty much a home-grown thing until the middle of the nineteenth century. By the twentieth century, the big three—Proctor & Gamble, Unilever, and Colgate—had 85 percent of the market, giving us not only detergents—which use fatty alcohols instead of animal fats—but also soap operas to carry their advertising.

During the Great Depression and into the years of World War II, housewives struggling to make ends meet would save their soap slivers, mixing the strong laundry soaps like Fels Naptha with the tongue-shaped remnants of Palmolive and Ivory and Lifebouy, pressing them together in a Soap Saver to swish through a sink full of hot water to make enough suds to do dishes. It was an indication of a family's good fortune and general economic gain when she could turn on a dishwasher and just throw the soap slivers away.

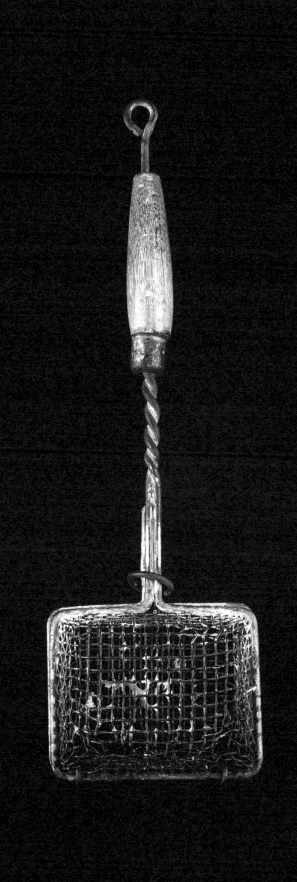

DISH RAG

This may look to you like a common, ordinary dishcloth. And you would be right, of course. To me, it also looks like a Native American woman wrapped in a blanket, in the style of the late Southwest artist R.C. Gorman. But that's just me. The point is that this common, ordinary dishcloth can take on different meanings to different folks. For instance, in our house, it is a Bone of Contention.

"You're not going to embarrass me, are you?" Marty, asks.

"Wouldn't dream of it," I say. And have to rethink how I'm going to present this piece.

The problem is that I once read that a dishcloth has the most germs of anything in the house. More germs than the toilet. As many as 4 billion *living* germs. All cohabitating merrily in the warm, moist comfort of the cloth sitting beside the kitchen sink. Here, insert a large *Yuk!*

Now, Marty is an intelligent woman. Presented with the facts, she can see the dangers. The problem is Grandma Beard. Grandma Beard always used a dishcloth. And to admit that Grandma Beard—paragon of all things clean, patron saint of Murphy's Oil Soap—could have actually spread germs rather than eradicate them is hard to accept. In matters of cleanliness in our house, one does not go lightly against the memory of Grandma Beard. (If you're beginning to hear an Annie Hall–type ring to this, you're not far off.)

However, Marty is also a reasonable woman. She is quick to point out—rightly so—that the dishcloth in the photograph isn't hers, that hers are all new and in good condition. (In fact it came from my mother-in-law, the Legendary Chub; why is this not a comfort?) And Marty changes dishcloths regularly, zapping them at times in the microwave. But still. Each time I see her wipe the cloth over the drainboard or dining room table, I cringe. Each watermark like the tracers of germ bullets. The contrail of a guided missile of disease aimed at my immune system.

"You know," she says sweetly, "if you don't like the way I do it, you could always . . ." And nods toward the paper towels.

SMALL WRINGER

It's a matter of scale. You probably think this a full-sized, mount-on-the-side-of-a-wash-tub wringer, large enough to wring the water from a sheet or tablecloth. But appearances, as we've noted, can be open to interpretation. It's actually only six inches wide and little more than that high, almost toy-like, meant not necessarily for the laundry room but for the kitchen (hence its inclusion in a collection of kitchen things) or wherever it was needed, able to be clamped on the side of a dishpan or sink to squeeze the water from more delicate, hand-washed items, such as ladies gloves or scarves as well as everyday dishcloths.

Wringers should more accurately be called squeezers, reflecting the difference between the act of wringing, which involves twisting, and squeezing, which involves pressing. (In England, a wringer is called a mangle; both here and abroad the word *mangle* is also the name of a large machine with heated rollers used for pressing clothes or household linens, though in either application the only thing that actually gets mangled is one's hand if one is not careful.) The hand-crank wringer appeared in America in the mid-1860s, though the washing machines to which they were attached were little more than tubs mounted on legs or wheels. The first electric washing machines had motorized wringers, though eventually the development of the spin cycle made them obsolete. Electric mangles are still found in professional laundries, and smaller home versions are popular in Europe.

When I was growing up in the 1940s and '50s, my mother had an electric mangle—the only one I'm sure in all of Beaver Falls, Pennsylvania. Once a week she sat down in front of it like an organist before a Wurlitzer, expertly nudging the controls with her knee as she rolled out freshly ironed sheets and table-cloths—and, just to show off a bit, my father's white dress shirts.

"My! If I only had an Anchor Brand Wringer."

"We Sell 'Em"

H. D. THOMPSON & CO., MALONE, N. Y.

Will call about_____

CLOTHESLINE REEL

"Aren't you stretching it a bit?"

"Stretching it," I say. "A clothesline. Clever."

Marty The Literal looks puzzled until she realizes the connection, then shrugs.

"You know what I mean. Is a clothesline really a kitchen thing?"

"Remember, I found it in my mother's kitchen, when I cleaned out the house."

"Your mother had everything even without the kitchen sink in her kitchen."

"True." The Sheriff—as my mother was affectionately known in her later years to my then-wife and California friends—had a thing about saving things. Boxes of Jell-O and butterscotch pudding from the '40s; skillets with their own built-in layer of grease; silverware from every free offer ever tended. Even the cat's pan. A panoply of smells—don't go there! "It's in our kitchen, too."

"As a decorator item," Marty says.

True again. The rationale for including it was that the reel was portable, that the line was probably strung only when it was needed to dry kitchen towels and dishcloths. I also simply like it. The form of it, the idea of it. Its textures, how it's aged. The juxtaposition, almost contradiction, of that tassel hanging down. Like a horse's mane or tail. The cowl of hair of a blonde-haired woman.

But maybe that's all there is to it. Maybe this collection of kitchen things is only a refinement of the same impulse that drove The Sheriff to not throw out chipped glassware and cracked plates and handless knives. What are we talking about, really? An attempt to hold on to this ever-fleeting world. To grasp this second of time and never let it go. To have it forever. To be able to look at it forever. Either in the form of an antique clothesline reel—or a photograph of it.

"You're thinking about your mother's house again, aren't you?"

"How did you know?"

"Your eye is doing that twitching thing."

CLOTHESPINS

If you've followed along with me this far, I'm sure you've guessed that I see these as more than a handful of clothespins held together by a rubber band. That's what happens if you travel in the realm of metaphors; things are always more than they seem. But there's a basis for this line of thinking in both Western and Eastern philosophy and speculations of how we know the things of this ever-fleeting world. For instance, I never expected to have the occasion to quote Immanuel Kant, but here he is in *The Transcendental Aesthetic*: "In general, nothing which is intuited in space is a thing in itself, and that space is not a form which belongs as a property to things. . . . Objects are quite unknown to us in themselves . . . [they are] mere representations of our sensibility."

That statement has more to do than just the evocative nature of a photograph; it's talking about the entire nature of reality, of the nature of things before the photograph is made, and how we know the things of the world—if we can indeed ever know them at all. In *The Republic*, Plato says that the average man and woman never see the objects of the worlds themselves; we see only the shadows of these objects as if they are projected on the wall of caves in which our perceptions hold us prisoners. One way of interpreting this analogy is that experience teaches us the general classification of things—chair, cat, clothespin—and when we see an object that coincides with a certain form, we make the recognition and call a spade a spade, as it were. Be that as it may, contemporary quantum physics turns this idea on its head and theorizes that it's just the opposite, that reality—not its shadow—takes place on a distant boundary surface, and everything we see in our everyday spatial dimensions is a projection of those faraway goings-on, like some super hologram. And these are just a few of such theories. So what is reality, what is real, and where is it? And where does that leave a humble picture of said reality, whose reality itself can be questioned?

Marty leans in over my shoulder. "That's an awful lot to . . . *pin* on a lit'l ol' image, don'tcha think?" Her laughter follows her out of the room like the off-key tinkle of a Good Humor truck.

ROUND MOUSETRAP

"Build a better mousetrap, and the world will beat a path to your door." Ralph Waldo Emerson, right? Well, not exactly. What Emerson actually said in his journal in 1855 is this: "If a man has good corn or wood, or boards, or pigs, to sell, or can make better chairs or knives, crucibles or church organs, than anybody else, you will find a broad hard-beaten road to his house, though it be in the woods." The popular version of the quote came along nearly thirty-five years later—seven years after the man died—when two women in preparing for a lecture tried to remember what Emerson said. Rather than take the time to look it up, they came up with this paraphrase. "If a man can write a better book, preach a better sermon, or make a better mousetrap than his neighbor, though he builds his house in the woods, the world will make a beaten path to his door." Well, close enough. Time and hearsay gave us the quote we wanted regardless.

The pursuit of The Better Mousetrap seems to be a fixation with Americans. Mousetraps are the most frequently invented device in the history of the US Patent and Trademark Office, with more than 4,400 patents issued to date—and growing—to say nothing of the thousands of applications that are turned down. All this to thwart the insidious natural instincts of the common house mouse, or in its official name (I love this), *Mus musculus*. Originally from Asia, mice were in the Mediterranean Basin by 8000 BC and throughout Europe by 1000 BC. In some way our tiny doppelganger, mice go wherever people go, living off our leavings while carrying diseases to kill us.

Mousetraps appear in Western literature as early as 1602, when Shakespeare's Hamlet gives it as the name of his play-within-a-play. The one pictured here wasn't The Better Mousetrap, though from the number that turn up in antique shops and flea markets, they must have been popular at one time. Of note is the fact that it was another product of the Lovell Company of Erie, Pennsylvania, who we saw earlier as the maker of Anchor Brand Wringers. In keeping with the spirit ascribed to Emerson's quote, Lovell apparently kept looking for those special products that click with consumers.

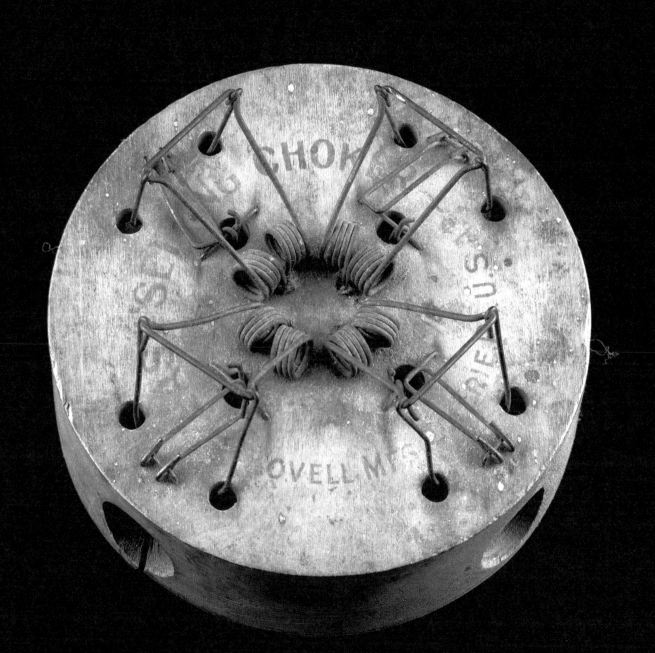

GRISWOLD SKILLET

Bill met the Legendary Chub when he was testing milk at the White Family Farm and she was home from college. Later, when he saw her at the Washington County Fair, he asked her to ride the Ferris Wheel, and a romance began in that swinging basket. Afterward, he would stop in to see her when she worked at The Shantee, the restaurant the family ran in conjunction with the farm, because it was a good way to get to know her, and flirt with her, without the local God-fearing church folk tucking her back into the folds of righteousness.

Their prospects weren't all that good, but they vowed to make a go of it. For a wedding present, they were given a calf, which seems quaint now, but at the time was quite a thing. It also sent a clear message as to which trail the Whites expected their new son-in-law to take. Accordingly, Bill and Chub settled in a small cement block home on the hill above the farm where they started their own family, living there in one room until they could afford to build a proper home over the hill. Not a farmhouse, mind you—Bill didn't have the heart physically to be a farmer, but he kept close to farm life, among other things inseminating cows and raising Bluetick hounds—but close enough for the kids to take a walk down the lane to their grandparents' house every day. Which is why Marty has mixed emotions to this day about the beauties and hardships of life on a farm.

The day they returned from their honeymoon at Niagara Falls, Bill bundled Chub in their pickup truck and drove into Hickory to Alison Brothers Hardware, where she picked out their first kitchen thing: this square iron skillet. When Chub dug it out of the basement for me to photograph, she said proudly, "It's a Griswold." She also said it was great for making grilled cheese sandwiches, which was about all she knew how to cook when they started.

GRISWOLD DAMPER

A cast-iron damper. A cast-iron Valentine as it were, straight through a collector's heart.

A damper, in case you were never exposed to such a thing, was/is used in the flue (the exhaust pipe) of a wood stove, to close off the stovepipe to keep birds and weather out, as well as to regulate the amount of air available to control the rate of combustion. (Lighting a wood fire with the damper closed is a smoky affair.) But that's not what's of interest about this particular damper. On the back, in raised characters, is this particular legend:

Griswold

Erie, PA., U.S.A.

American

4 IN

and barely discernible, 523. Yes, like the Legendary Chub's cherished skillet, it's a Griswold.

The cast-iron cookware of the Griswold Manufacturing Company has attained celebrated status among collectors, in the same way that it was once prized among cooks and housewives. From 1865 to 1957, Griswold achieved worldwide recognition for the quality of its cookware, for instance, winning five awards in the 1893 World's Fair. In fact, Griswold turned out a full line of cast-iron items, including fireplace sets, cuspidors, umbrella stands, and muffin pans. And dampers.

Eventually Griswold succumbed to its own corporate weight. A curious thing about companies: that as the number of employees grow, the amount of profit per employee shrinks; that the efficiencies of scale of corporate growth are almost always outweighed by the burden of its growing bureaucracy. First Griswold was bought out by its main competitor, Wagner, then both were eventually swallowed into a conglomerate. Both Griswold and Wagner cookware are made today, and both are highly regarded, but, like with people, the ones that are preferred tend to be experienced and well-seasoned.

MATCH HOLDER

Once at a photography workshop in Virginia City, Nevada, an otherwise perceptive, intelligent gentleman (he was a professor of genetics at UC Davis, as I recall) came trotting past, his view camera and tripod slung over his shoulder, shouting to me joyously as he headed toward the rear of an abandoned mine building, "Peeling paint, a cracked window, *and* a spider's web!" What is it about photography that it finds an affinity with the deteriorating and the used? The aging and the falling apart? Maybe it's the fact that a photograph is the record of a moment of time, and as such is in the process of aging and deteriorating even as we look at it. In the words of the German poet, Rainer Maria Rilke, "O quickly disappearing photograph / In my more slowly disappearing hand."

For those of you of the digital age, this fellow is a matchbox holder, designed to hang on the wall and hold an entire box of matches, close at hand to a wood stove or gas range back in the days before pilot lights, ready for the matches to be scooped out of the open tray as needed to light kindling or a burner. Matches in some form or another have been around since ancient Rome and China, though in Europe into the 1800s, steel, flint, and tinder were still used to make fire. Phosphorus matches were created in the 1830s, but they needed special containers because they could ignite against any surface, often violently, and had to be kept away from the air. In 1844, the Swedish invented the safety match, though the term is confusing today because it's used indiscriminately for the safety match and the strike-anywhere match. The true safety match separates the active ingredients between the match head and a special surface on the side of the box; the strike-anywhere match combines the active ingredients so the match can be ignited . . . er, anywhere. Matches kept in the type of tin pictured here were usually of the strike-anywhere variety.

Having maintained his position on the wall at the White Family Farm since the early 1900s, this old fellow is sinking rapidly beyond character into decrepitude. Flakey. Forgetful of what he was supposed to hold in the first place. I just wish he'd keep his teeth in and go out with a little dignity.

SOAP DISH

"That's exactly like what I was telling you about."

"What were you telling me about?"

"The bugs."

"What bugs?"

"The ones on my grandparents' farm."

"This is a soap dish."

"There were centipedes just like that, and millipedes, and silverfish, crawling all over the place. You couldn't pick up a bucket or jar in the barn without one scuttling away."

"They probably weren't just like this. They would have to be proportionally thinner, and about one-eighth the length, if that. And this can't scuttle anywhere; it's a soap dish."

"People say, 'Oh, you were raised on a farm,' like it's a badge of honor, they think it's so great, like I'm closer to the earth or something. Well, let me tell you, the good old days and back to the earth meant a lot of bugs and things crawling on you you don't want to know about."

"I never accused you of being closer to the earth. . . ."

"And spiders, you wouldn't believe. The ones I really hated were the jumping kind. Little black spiders, you could see the fur on them. You think one is just walking along and then all of a sudden—*Whoops!* It jumps three feet into your hair or on your dress or something."

"There is no recorded incident, I'm sure, of a soap dish jumping into somebody's hair. . . ."

"They'd hide in the grass, the grass would be full of them, and my grandparents rarely cut the grass close to the house. Grandpap would always say he had more important things to do, but you couldn't go around the side of the house without them jumping on you."

"Marty, this is a soap dish."

She looks at me like I'm deranged. "Well, of course. I know that. What did you think?"

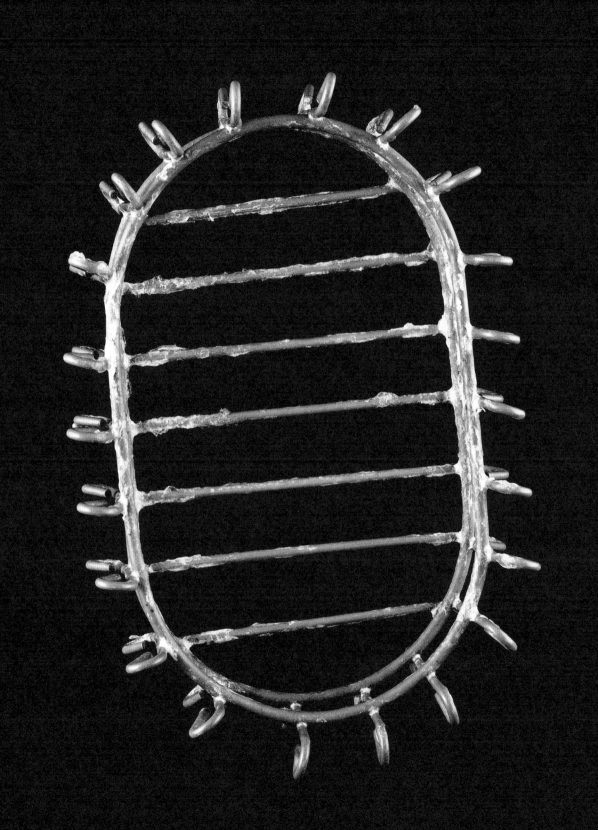

FANNIE FOX COOKBOOK

It would have made such a great story: the actual cookbook that the Legendary Chub used to become Legendary. True, this is the cookbook her mother used until Great Aunt Mary E took over the kitchen. Then it dropped out of sight until it came time to clean out the farmhouse after the property was sold. The Legendary Chub actually learned to cook with the help of Betty Crocker.

Recipes have been written down since the time of the Babylonians and Egyptians; Kublai Khan's chef collected his favorites into a treatise called *The Important Things to Know about Eating and Drinking*. Until the eighteenth century, European cookbooks were written by men, which coincided with the growth of cooking as an applied art to be practiced only by professionals. Then women began publishing cookbooks for housewives—most notably in America were those of Mary J. Lincoln and Fannie Farmer—but they were often more like kitchen bibles, dispensing advice as well as recipes.

Fannie Fox was the sister of popular novelist Edna Ferber (*Show Boat, Giant*) who wrote the foreword for Fannie's cookbook. In it she remembers a cookbook from their childhood, *Aunt Babette's Cook Book*, whose "pages bore frescoes, dadoes, and thumb marks of chocolate, flour, lemon juice . . . splashes of yolks, such as ornament any cook book in common use." But Edna, and by inference Fannie, felt "something like horror" at the "wanton waste" of the earlier recipes. *Babette's*, though not kosher, was written for socially aspiring Jewish women of the Gilded Age. Fannie's, by contrast, "is a book for the modern, intelligent, and capable woman (or one who wishes to be); to whom her kitchen and table are important but not all-important; who can have guests without undue flurry; manage her housekeeping budget in a businesslike manner." Mary Lydia Downie White, who was the first woman in Hickory, Pennsylvania, to wear pants *and* a beret, must have felt that description fit her perfectly.

Chocolate Nut Pudding

1 cup bread crumbs	1 teaspoon grated lemon rind
1 cup chopped nuts	2 squares chocolate
2 egg yolks	2 cups hot milk
¾ cup sugar	¼ teaspoon salt
1 tablespoon lemon juice	2 egg whites

Beat the egg yolks in the sugar, add the crumbs, nuts, lemon juice and rind, the hot milk, and melted chocolate. Lastly fold in the stiffly beaten egg whites. Pour the pudding into buttered ramekins or molds and bake it twenty-five minutes in a moderate oven. Serve it hot with Custard Sauce or cream.

Cocoanut Bread Pudding

2 cups bread crumbs	⅔ cup sugar
4 cups warm milk	1 teaspoon baking powder
1 tablespoon melted butter	1 can Baker's coconut
2 egg yolks	2 egg whites
	Vanilla

Heat milk, stir in butter and sugar, add crumbs and other ingredients and last the egg whites beaten stiffly. Add vanilla.

Date Bread Pudding

½ cup dates	½ cup nuts
1 cup bread	2 eggs
2 tablespoons sugar	½ cup milk

Put stoned dates, nuts, and bread through the grinder. Add eggs, sugar, and milk. Bake half an hour. Serve with cream.

Prune Bread Pudding

1½ cups stewed sweetened prunes	½ teaspoon cinnamon
Bread Pudding recipe (page 241)	

Prepare the Bread Pudding as usual. Put a layer of prunes in a well-buttered baking dish. Pour on half the pudding, then lay on another layer of prunes. Sprinkle them with cinnamon and pour on the remainder of the Bread Pudding. Bake it in a moderate oven as for Bread Pudding and serve it with the juice from the stewed prunes.

Brown Betty

3 cups sliced or chopped apples	½ cup water
2 cups fresh bread crumbs	1 teaspoon cinnamon
½ cup brown sugar	3 tablespoons butter
¼ teaspoon nutmeg	Rind and juice of 1 lemon

Mix apples with the crumbs, sugar, cinnamon, and nutmeg. Add the butter melted and place in buttered pudding dish. Pour the water, lemon juice, and rind over this. Cover with crumbs and butter and bake in moderate oven for forty-five minutes. Serve with Hard Sauce or jelly.

Corn Flake Brown Betty

2 cups corn flakes	Apples
1½ tablespoons butter	Brown sugar
Raisins	

Butter a baking pan well. Put in a layer of corn flakes. Core and pare the apples and slice them thin. Place a layer of apples and raisins over the corn flakes and then a layer of brown sugar. Continue this until the dish is filled, having the brown sugar on the top. Bake in a moderate oven. Serve this with jelly and Foamy Sauce or cream.

Apple Pudding with Brown Sugar

6 medium-sized apples	1 cup hot water
1 tablespoon lemon juice	½ cup flour
3 tablespoons sugar	½ cup butter
1 teaspoon cinnamon	1 cup brown sugar

Pare the apples and slice them thin. Place them in a buttered baking dish, alternating the apple layers with the lemon juice, white sugar, and cinnamon. Pour half the water over them and let them stand thirty minutes. Then add the remainder of the water. Mix the flour and sugar and add the melted butter. The mixture will be crumbly. Put this over the apples and bake in a slow oven about forty minutes. Serve cool with whipped cream or plain cream.

Sponge and Apple Pudding

1 egg cake recipe (page 338)	4 apples
Whipping cream	

Butter a deep pudding dish and line with the apples, which have been peeled, cored, and halved. Pour the cake batter over. Bake half an hour and serve with whipped cream.

COFFEEPOT

Because of the pervasiveness of advertising, I tend to associate coffee—when I associate it with anything beyond where my next cup is coming from—with Brazil or maybe Colombia, with a manly looking peasant in a serape and a nice burro, happily harvesting coffee for the rest of the world's enjoyment. Oh sure, I've heard of Kona coffee from Hawaii, and Starbucks foists Ethiopian and Arabica blends on me at times, but overall there is Juan Valdez and his burro. (Yes, I know how terribly, terribly wrong that portrayal is.) In fact, South America produces about half the world's coffee. But how it got there is a story in itself.

Legend has it that coffee was discovered by a Ethiopian shepherd boy in the ninth century who noticed his goats were particularly frisky when they ate the red berries of a certain tree. But the story is apocryphal. We do know that coffee drinking was documented in Yemen and Arabia in the fifteenth century and a century later had spread to the rest of the Middle East, Persia, Turkey, and Africa. From there, it went to Italy and the rest of Europe, Indonesia, and the Americas. The Dutch in the seventeenth century were the main suppliers of coffee to the rest of Europe, and then did a curious thing: in 1714 they gave a cutting to the French king, Louis XIV, who cultivated it in the royal garden. A few years later, a young naval officer obtained a seedling and, despite a horrendous journey worthy of a Steve McQueen movie, transported it to Martinique. In fifty years, it propagated more than eighteen million coffee trees. Eventually its progeny spread throughout the Caribbean, South and Central America, and today provides 90 percent of the world's coffee.

Quite a journey for the cells of that one little cutting, trickling down through the centuries to find themselves in the basket of this humble percolator—scratched and dented, splattered with paint from the time they redid the kitchen—bubbling along on top of the stove in the early morning light as Marty's grandfather, John White, stands at the window looking out over his fields, then turns to pour his first cup for the day, reaching toward the handle as if to shake the hand of an old friend.

TEA BALL

John White, farmer, rugged individualist, fiercely American, living in the middle years of the twentieth century, would have left drinking tea to the ladies. Considering it something slightly effeminate, certainly not a man's drink; considering tea as something to be served at a woman's club luncheon, something you'd drink if you were Asian or English. Slightly un-American. Definitely suspicious.

America probably would be more of a tea-drinking nation—we started out that way, being a British colony, though tea was originally brought to America by the Dutch—except for the Boston Tea Party. In reaction to an expensive cargo of tea being dumped in Boston harbor to protest high taxes, the British sent troops to clamp down on the city and a revolution was born; drinking tea was seen as supporting "the oppressors," drinking coffee a blow for freedom. Tea was first discovered, so the story goes, by China's second Emperor, Shen Nung, in 2737 BC when some dry leaves from a camellia bush blew into his cup of hot water. It was considered a medicinal beverage until 300 AD when it became more of a daily drink. A few centuries later, tea was introduced to Japan when Buddhist monks studying in China returned home and brought seeds and leaves with them. In the 1600s, the Dutch East India Company marketed tea as an exotic medicinal drink, but it was so expensive only the very rich could afford it and the serving pieces to go with it. In the same period, Russia signed a treaty with China that brought the tea trade across Mongolia and Siberia; eventually tea, along with vodka, became Russia's national drink. Definitely un-American.

Today, tea is said to be the world's most popular drink next to water. Tea-drinking in America is steadily increasing because we link it with a good-health, clean-environment lifestyle; we drink 140 million cups a day, 80 percent in the form of iced tea. The preferred drink of business lunches, now that martinis are frowned upon, to show that one is a responsible person. Beyond suspicion.

CINNAMON BEAR

"So, why the picture of the cinnamon bear? That's what we called this guy when I was growing up. 'I need the cinnamon bear for my toast.' Oh, I get it. It's to talk about cinnamon. I read somewhere that cinnamon is the most popular smell in the world, next to vanilla. Is that it?"

"No, not really. . . ."

"Then maybe it's to talk about sugar. One of your set pieces—you've got the form down to a science—where sugar comes from, how it's cut and processed. That would be interesting."

"No. . . ."

"Okay then. Maybe it's to demonstrate the use of animal imagery in food packaging. I've always wondered where that idea came from? Bears for sweet things, honey and syrup and . . ."

I shrug, shake my head. "I'm not really sure at this point why I took the photograph. It could have been any of those things, or none of them. All I know for sure is that there was something about it that made me want to take it. I used to think I took a photograph to try to find out what it was about a subject that would make me want to go through the effort to take its image. Then I thought it was tied to what we learn about the observer in quantum mechanics. The idea that looking at a thing changes it, that I wanted to change the subject by making a photograph of it and in that way make it mine. Or for that matter, maybe it was just the simple human desire to hold on to some part of this ever-fleeting world. But now I'm beginning to think it's even more basic. That it's wrapped up in the whole business of consciousness and Schrödinger's cat."

"Schrödinger's cat," Marty says.

"It's as if taking a photograph is analogous to the act of consciousness itself. That consciousness not only changes and defines the physical world, but is necessary to create it."

"Who's Schrödinger? And why should I care about his cat? Was it a rescue animal?"

"One certainly hopes so."

MEAT TENDERIZER

"Schrödinger set up a facetious situation to show the contradictions in one interpretation of quantum theory in regard to an observer. Purely as a thought experiment, he put a cat in a sealed box with a radioactive source, a vial of poison, and a Geiger counter rigged to a hammer."

"His name was Schrödinger? It sounds like a Rube Goldberg device to me."

I ignore her and go on. "If a single atom decays in an hour's time, the Geiger counter will detect it, which will trip the hammer to break the vial to release the poison and kill the cat. The Copenhagen interpretation of quantum mechanics said that until an outcome of an event is observed, it exists in all possible states of existence at once. In this case, because the box is sealed, we can't know if the cat is dead or alive, so the cat is said to be both alive and dead. Until we open the box."

"Well, that's just silly."

"In a way, Schrödinger meant it to be, though it raised an important issue about the role of the observer. For years it was used as an example of how observing an event changes it. But it turned out to reinforce that there are many possibilities or probabilities about a thing until you observe or measure it. Which inadvertently reinforced the necessity of a consciousness to make it real. Some scientists get around it by saying there are different realities, we're seeing one reality and someone in another reality is seeing another. To us, the cat is alive, to the other the cat is dead."

Marty-of-the-Here-And-Now shakes her head. "And is this the hammer in the sealed box?"

"No, that's a meat tenderizer."

"So what does it have to do with Schrödinger's cat?"

"Nothing, actually. Though I guess according to quantum mechanics, you could say it is both a meat tenderizer and the hammer in Schrödinger's experiment. We don't know which one it is until we see it in use."

"I think it's time to get a grip."

LONG-NECKED GRIPPER

Grips we have. Though to one of an active imagination, and one thinking of multiple interpretations of reality, this image of a giraffe-necked, sexually-aroused gripper isn't much help.

Getting a grip would be easier if we knew for a certainty there was actually something outside of ourselves to get a grip of. But it seems it's not that easy. Broken down to its smallest particles, the substance of the world isn't there at all; matter turns out to be a dance of energy, particles we can't see and are not always able to prove exist at all in a whirl of varying stages of decay and chaos. It's not a new idea, actually. Lucretius, a spooky guy, sitting in his toga in the middle years of the first century BC, reasoned that infinitely small particles called atoms form together to make things as we know them and then dissipate in time. Two thousand years later, experiments show that those atoms are made of electrons that are both particle and wave, but how and where such particles (or waves) are located depend upon the act of observation. To say nothing of what's called dark matter, which could be the fabric that holds the rest of our known world together.

The world we know is a description that we tell to ourselves. We know the shapes and colors and forms of our kitchen because photons of light bounce off our kitchen things and interact with the pulses of our brains. But light has no color or form on its own; it's only electromagnetic radiation. It takes a brain, a consciousness, to assemble it. Which raises the question: When a consciousness isn't present, do those kitchen things still exist? If that weren't question enough, there is evidence that we don't live in a universe, we are part of a multiverse, with realities piled up or strung out on realities, and the constants upon which our science is based—for instance, that light travels at a speed of 299,792,458 meters per second and that nothing is faster—aren't necessarily constant in those other realities. Get a grip indeed. Got any ideas how? Or where?

CHOPPER

Space and time, as quantum and post-quantum theories demonstrate, are constructs of the mind; they are the tools that the mind uses to give a framework for our internal description of the world we think we experience. The mind takes the waves of probability that assault our senses and converts them through neural activity into our 3D experience of the world. That's true for sight and sound and smells—but it's true for touch as well. My whirls of subatomic energy that define my physical limits touching upon your whirls of subatomic energy or those that I've learned to call a chair. The kicker is that the same is true of dreams; they too are the result of neural activity, the same neural activity that takes its stimulation from our waking hours, so which can be said to be the more real? And metaphors are a kind of waking dream, spanning the two realities.

Take, as an example, this image of a chopping knife. I know it's a chopping knife because I've learned through experience and my particular culture the words *chopping knife* identify this shape and form— and yet this particular shape and form sets off other associations in my particular mind. The first thing it reminds me of is a Japanese gate or *Torii* that marks the entrance to a Shinto shrine. In stark contrast, this chopping knife also makes me think of a stick-figure woman reaching down to lift the hem of her hoop skirt. And it reminds me of a puppy with its paws hanging down over a barrier—or, a more personal image, the way our tuxedo cat Frankie leans over the top of her tall perch in the living room, looking down at the goings-on below. I'm also reminded that this kitchen thing was sent to me by my friend Linda, and for the briefest instant, I am once again standing with her in the kitchen of her house in San Anselmo as she makes us strong coffee, talking of photographs and photographers, the green sunlight filtering in through the bushes outside.

All of it real and none of it real. All this from a photograph, which itself is a description, a description of a description, if you will, and this isn't even the original photograph, but a copy on a printed page, a description of a description of a description. It's enough to give you a headache.

ALUMINUM PITCHER

Quantum mechanics finished off what Copernicus started, namely that we are not the focus point of the universe. Or are we? Because quantum theories and experiments make one thing terribly and inextricably clear: the role of the observer is indispensable. That's you and me. And the universe—at least this universe, the level of reality in which we find ourselves—shows every indication of having evolved for the purpose of consciousness. As the late physicist John Archibald Wheeler, the man who named black holes, said, "We are participators in bringing into being not only the near and here but the far away and long ago. We are in this sense, participators in bringing about something of the universe . . ." The observer is everything; we are in effect here to observe, and in the process create the world we live in. And what we see mainly are things. Such as this milk pitcher.

These stamped aluminum pitchers were a common item in households and diners during the 1930s and '40s. Marked on its base *Priscilla Ware Speaks for Itself*, it was a product of the depression years when aluminum companies, to fight the bad economy and foreign competition, introduced thin-wall kitchen-ware—a two-and-a-half-quart pitcher like this sold for around twenty cents. This particular pitcher was used for many years on the White Farm; Marty remembers it sitting on the table in the dining room of her grandparents' house, filled with cold milk from the springhouse. In my mind, it conjures up an image of a summer afternoon, the long dining room table crowded with family and field hands sitting down to lunch, her grandfather saying a blessing, her grandmother keeping an eye on the hands; an image of Marty walking barefoot in the grass, carrying this pitcher of milk to the house, her brother and sister trailing behind, the buzz of honeybees and dragonflies along the creek bank. You will have your own images, of course. The glory and necessity of consciousness.

Things have their own stories and images. Cezanne knew. "People imagine a sugar bowl has no face, no soul. But it changes every day. You have to know how to get hold of these fellows . . . These glasses, those plates, they talk to each other, they're constantly telling confidences."

FUNNELS

"I can see where you're going with this."

"That's good."

"Circles within circles."

"Yeah. . . ."

". . . worlds within worlds, realities within realities . . ."

"Well, sort of. . . ."

"And you're coming toward the end of the book. Funneling down to a conclusion."

"Hmm. Well, actually I was first interested in the funnels themselves and how to show the two of them together. I wasn't really thinking anything else. That I was aware of."

Marty gives me a Marty look. "You're the one who got me thinking this way. Looking for metaphors, associations that open up interpretations. And now you're telling me something else?"

"No, you're right. All of those associations are there. I'm just thinking that I don't want to get too far away from the importance of the thing itself. Just as a thing. A couple of funnels. They're really important just the way they are."

"I'm getting a headache."

"I had one a few pages ago. Thinking about other universes, other realities."

"So, now you're changing your story?"

"No. It's the same story. I just don't want to lose sight of the main characters."

"Because, as long as you're pursuing this 'story' analogy, there's a problem with some of these 'stories' you've been telling. About the farm and the Legendary Chub. And me."

"Such as?"

"Such as, they're not always true."

"And you see that as a problem?"

FAMILY TRIVET

"There's nothing trivial about a trivet."

"Nice line."

"Anything that puts itself in the way of something else getting scorched or burned qualifies as a hero in some realities. It could tell quite a story. Particularly with the photographs of you and your brother and sister. . . ."

"Are we back to other realities?"

"No, I meant a story in this reality. A story in just this image."

"Because there's that problem that not all of your stories are true."

"Such as?"

"Well, I never walked barefoot in the grass to bring cold milk up from the springhouse."

"Okay, but it could have happened."

"Yes, I suppose . . ."

"And it makes a point. It's a nice image. The bees and dragonflies buzzing around, the springhouse and the creek."

"Yes, I suppose."

"It's an image in the mind. In the same way that this image of the trivet is an image in the mind. We make our reality, though we're never aware we're doing it. And one is as true as another."

"Or as false."

"True. For that matter they could all be true—or false—in a separate reality. Who's to say? The important thing is the thing itself. That we perceive there are things out there real or unreal, with stories to tell, true or false. We have to hold to those things. Because they're all we have."

"Of course, it's more complicated in that most of these conversations never took place."

"But they could have. Just because a story is false doesn't make it any less true."

STRAINER WITH EARS

Maybe the act of photographing a thing mirrors the act of consciousness itself. Before a thing is looked at—that is, before it's observed by a conscious mind—it exists on the subatomic level only as waves of probability; then the act of being seen collapses its wave-functions so it assumes a particular place or motion. As Nobel physicist John Wheeler noted, "No phenomenon is a real phenomenon until it is an observed phenomenon." In a similar way, photographing a subject stops the wave of all the possible or probable images we could take of the subject and it assumes a particular place or motion. Instead of remembering all of that special afternoon with the sunlight through the leaves of the trees and the picnic on the grass with a person we love, we remember the photograph we took of it—the particular in the wave of possibilities and probabilities; and in that act of observing, change the moment forever—a day filled with however many different conflicting emotions, the concern for that unfamiliar noise coming from the transmission on the drive to that isolated spot, the hurt feelings when the loved one talked too much about someone else, the thousand worries and uncertainties that beset us each and every day, collapsed by that isolated image into one shining laughing forever moment.

"So we're back to all this wave and particle stuff," Marty says. "You know I don't believe it."

"It's been proven hundreds of times. Maybe thousands . . ."

"Then I should rephrase it. It's not that I don't believe it; it's more that I just don't care."

"But I think it's important to consider, it's how we know our world."

Marty bats her eyes. "I have to tell you: I believe the kitchen is downstairs where I left it, even though I'm not there to look at it."

"What can I tell you?" I shrug. Tight-lipped, befitting a hapless Stan Laurel.

"Though I guess I would agree," Marty laughs, "that when I'm in the kitchen, it's a better place for it."

SMALL MILK PAIL

"What did you mean, 'Things are all we have?'"

"Well, it seems like that. Things are what we know of the world. And they're important to us. They define us, they tell us who we are. I remember the news story of a sick little girl in the Sudan. She had been carried to an aid station, but there was no room for her and they left her lying on the ground. As she lay there in rags dying, she fingered a red string bracelet on her wrist that her father had made for her. It was the only *thing* she had in the world. It was everything to her."

"But that's not a story about a thing. It's about a person. People. And the stories about things in this book, these things don't come alive until you talk about the people who used them. Besides, a thing can't do this." She leans over and kisses me before heading back downstairs to the kitchen. Very pleased with herself. And I have to admit it's a convincing argument.

When I found this milk pail in the Legendary Chub's basement, it reminded me why I began this series. There was no physics here, no metaphysics, no metaphor, no other realities. It was an entity all of its own, and every knock and ping on the surface told its story. Beautiful in and of itself.

Yet I know now it only took on life when it took on other life, until I saw in my mind's eye (but then it's all in my mind's eye, just as it is for you in yours) this pail carried by a barefoot child up across the fields on a sunny afternoon, swinging it by the handle, the metal damp with sweat from the cold lemonade inside, through the tall grass to where her grandfather and a hand are bucking bales, loading them on the hay wagon, and as the two men take turns drinking from the can, she goes to the horse standing in the traces and pats its neck, running her hand up under its mane, the large brown eye watching her as it blinks a fly away, and then when the men are done and starting work again, she walks back across the fields, the wire handle of the empty pail squeaking now with every step, grasshoppers leaping ahead of her, down the hill again toward the house and the barn where her younger brother and sister play near the springhouse. All of a summer day. Worlds ago.

ACKNOWLEDGMENTS

A number of these photographs and essays—if essays are what you call them; stories may be more appropriate—first appeared, sometimes in a different form, in *TABLE* Magazine.

Many people have helped bring *Kitchen Things* to fruition. I hesitate to start naming names for fear of who I might inadvertently leave out. If I do forget to include someone, it's my failing, not yours—you know who you are. My thanks go to:

Linda Connor, for her early enthusiasm and on-going support; Brian Taylor and Alan McGee—or, Alan McGee and Brian Taylor—my collective photographic conscience; Christina French, for giving Kitchen Things their beautiful spreads in *TABLE Magazine*; Mark Rengers, who showed the images first on the walls of his Sewickley Gallery; Dave Meek, who willingly took on the role of Average Reader to help with proofing; Jack Ritchie, who shared some flea market adventures, once upon a time; JoAnn and Chip Cowden (and Adam, too, for that matter), as well as Marty's coworkers, Kathy Bruce, Gail Herlinger, and Bill Shuster, for lending me some family treasures; Chuck Zvirman, whose eyes lit up when I talked about including recipes in this series; Ron Arias, an unflinching wall to bounce things against since our days at Berkeley; Cheryl Haus, my uncommon friend and reader; Carol Snodgrass, who helped me learn to always keep my powder dry; Martha White, aka the Legendary Chub, who to her credit went against her better judgment; Nicole Frail, my editor at Skyhorse, who is everything an author could ask for and then some; Barbara Clark, my agent, for her unwavering support and faith lo these many years—my Audience of One; and, of course, as in all things, to Marty, my heart, who has never stopped believing, and is never shy in reminding me.

SOURCES AND RESOURCES

In doing research for the sections of text in this book, the first place I consulted, without fail, was Wikipedia. Without this incredible resource, this book would be a lot less informative. Here are some of the books that influenced me along the way, as well.

Alexander, Brian S. *Spiffy Kitchen Collectibles*. Iola: Krause Publications, 2003.

Brown, Bill, ed. *Things*. Chicago and London: The University of Chicago Press, 2004.

Busch, Akiko. *Geography of Home*. New York: Princeton Architectural Press, 1999.

Franklin, Linda Campbell. *300 Years of Kitchen Collectibles, 5th Edition*. Iola: Krause Publications, 2003.

Glenn, Joshua and Hayes, Carol. *Taking Things Seriously*. New York: Princeton Architectural Press, 2007.

Greene, Brian. *The Hidden Reality*. New York: Alfred A Knopf, 2011.

Gribbin, John. *In Search of Schrodinger's Cat: Quantum Physics and Reality*. Toronto, New York, London, Sydney, Auckland: Bantam Books, 1984.

Kaku, Michio. *Hyperspace*. New York, Oxford: Oxford University Press, 1994.

Kubler, George. *The Shape of Time: Remarks on the History of Things*. New Haven and London: Yale University Press, 1973.

Lanza, M.D., with Bob Berman. *Biocentrism*. Dallas: BenBella Books, 2009.

Lubar, Steven and Kingery, W. David, eds. *History From Things: Essays on Material Culture*. Washington and London: Smithsonian Institution Press, 1993.

Nelson, Victoria. *The Secret Life of Puppets*. Cambridge and London: Harvard University Press, 2001.

Norretranders, Tor. *The User Illusion: Cutting Consciousness Down to Size*. New York: Viking, 1998.

Prown, Jules David, and Haltman, Kenneth, eds. *American Artifacts: Essays in Material Culture*. East Lansing: Michigan State University Press, 2000.

Restak, M.D., Richard. *The Naked Brain: How the Emerging Neurosociety is Changing How We Live, Work, and Love*. New York: Three Rivers Press, 2006.

Thornton, Don. Beat This: *The Eggbeater Chronicles*. Sunnyvale: Off Beat Books, 1994.

Watson, Lyall. *The Nature of Things: The Secret Life of Inanimate Objects*. Rochester: Destiny Books, 1992

Zweig, C. Dianne. *Hot Kitchen and Home Collectibles of the 30s, 40s, and 50s*. Paducah: Collector Books, 2007.

Print and Internet Articles

"About Cake." The Food Timeline, accessed 2011, http://www.foodtimeline.org/foodcakes.html.

"About J.R.Watkins." J.R.Watkins, accessed 2010, http://www.jrwatkins.com/jrwatkins/contentF.cfm?Country=Usa&Area=Our%20Story&mainstg=Who%20We%20Are.

"About Vermont Maple Syrup." Vermont Maple Syrup, accessed 2010, http://www.vermontmaple.org/about.php.

"Alfred L. Cralle." Notable Pittsburgh Inventors, Carnegie Library. http://www.carnegielibrary.org/research/pittsburgh/patentees/cralle.html.

Alissa Hamilton. "Fresh Squeezed: The Truth About Orange Juice in Boxes." CivilEats.com, last modified 2010, accessed 2011, http://civileats.com/2010/01/25/getting-fresh-an-interview-with-alissa-hamilton-on-orange-juice.

"An Introduction to Cooking Pastry Including the Different Types." helpwithcooking.com, accessed 2010, http://www.helpwithcooking.com/pastry-guide/introduction-pastry.html.

"Antique Ice Cream Scoops." LoveToKnow.com, accessed 2011, http://antiques.lovetoknow.com/Antique_Ice_Cream_Scoops.

Audet, Marye. "50 Great Uses for Mason Jars." Care2, last modified 2009, accessed 2011, http://www.care2.com/greenliving/50-great-uses-for-mason-jars.html.

"A Brief History of American Cookbooks." Feeding America: The Historic American Cookbook Project, accessed 2011, http://digital.lib.msu.edu/projects/cookbooks/html/project.html.

"A Brief History of Common Home Canning Jars." PickYourOwn.org, accessed 2011, http://www.pickyourown.org/canningjars.htm.

"A Brief History of Pasta." World of Food and Wine, accessed 2011, http://www.world-food-and-wine.com/brief-history-pasta.

"A History of Tea Timeline." 2B A Snob, accessed 2011, http://2basnob.com/tea-history-timeline.html.

"A World History of Weights and Measures." Cool Fire Technology, accessed 2011, http://www.cftech.com/BrainBank/OTHERREFERENCE/WEIGHTSandMEASURES/MetricHistory.html.

"Bacon Nutrition Facts." Buzzle.com, accessed 2011, http://www.buzzle.com/articles/bacon-nutrition-facts.html.

Baer, Meryl. "Soap-Making Companies in the 1900s." eHow.com, accessed 2011, http://www.ehow.com/info_7757736_soapmaking-companies-1900s.html.

Batres-Marquez, S. Patricia, MS; Helen H. Jensen, PhD; Julie Upton, MS, RD. "Rice Consumption in the United States: Recent Evidence from Food Consumption Surveys." *Eat Right*. The American Dietetic Association, 2009, accessed 2010, http://www.usarice.com/doclib/229/4290.pdf.

Bayne, G.K. "How to Use Measuring Spoons and Cups." ehow.com, accessed 2011, http://www.ehow.com/how_2278953_use-measuring-spoons-cups.html.

Bellis, Mary. "The History of Matches." About.com.Inventors, accessed 2011, http://inventors.about.com/library/inventors/blmatch.htm.

Berning, Bill & Jan. "Collectibles-General (Antiques)/Columbia Family Scale." AllExperts, last modified 2007, accessed 2011, http://en.allexperts.com/q/Collectibles-General-Antiques-682/Columbia-Family-Scale-1.htm.

"Book Matches." The Great Idea Finder, accessed 2011, http://www.ideafinder.com/history/inventions/matches.htm.

Budnik, Paul. "Schrodinger's Cat." Mountain Math Software, accessed 2011, http://mtnmath.com/faq/meas-qm-3.html.

"Cake Recipe History." Recipes 4 Cakes, accessed 2011, http://wwwrecipes4cakes/cakehistory.

"Cakes – History of Cakes." What's Cooking America, accessed 2011, http://whatscookingamerica.net/History/CakeHistory.htm.

"Citrus Juice History." Google Search Timeline, accessed 2011, http://twurl.nl/epcvb3.

Clay, Jackie. "Canning 101." *Backwoods Home* Magazine, accessed 2011, http://www.backwoodshome.com/articles/clay53.html.

"Clothes Peg Making." Diverse Herts, accessed 2011, http://www.diverseherts.org.uk/archive_item.php?ArchiveID=254.

"Coffee History." CoffeerResearch.org, accessed 2011, http:// www.coffeeresearch.org/coffee/history.htm.

"Coffee History." Koffee Korner, accessed 2011, http://www.koffeekorner.com/koffeehistory.htm.

"Cookbook History." The Cook's Palate, accessed 2011, http://cookspalate.com/cookbook-history.htm.

Deutscher, Guy. "Does Your Language Shape How You Think?" *The New York Times* Magazine, accessed 2010, http://www.nytimes.com/2010/08/29/magazine/29language-t.html?scp=1&sq=GUY%20DEUTSCHER&st=cse.

"Directions for Home Water Bath Canning." PickYourOwn.org, accessed 2011, http://www.pickyourown.org/water_bath_canning.htm.

Dossey, Larry, "M.D. Is Consciousness the Center of the Universe?" Huffington Post, last modified 2010, accessed 2011. http://www.huffingtonpost.com.

"Encyclopedia of Spices: Nutmeg." the epicenter, accessed 2010, http://theepicentre.com/Spices/nutmeg.html.

Filippone, Peggy Trowbridge. "Bacon and Health." About.com, accessed 2011, http://www.about.com/od/pork/a/baconhealth.htm.

Filippone, Peggy Trowbridge. "Bacon Cooking Tips." About.com, accessed 2011, http://www.about.com/od/pork/a/bacontips.htm.

Filippone, Peggy Trowbridge. "Bacon History." About.com, accessed 2011, http://www.about.com/od/pork/a/baconhealth.htm.

Filippone, Peggy Trowbridge. "Coffee History." About.com: Home Cooking, accessed 2011, http://home-cooking.about.com/od/foodhistory/a/coffeehistory.htm.

Flippone, Peggy Trowbridge. "Nutmeg and Mace History." About.com, accessed 2010, http://homecooking.about.com/od/foodhistory/a/nutmeghistory.htm.

"Flour." JoyofBaking.com, accessed 2011, http://www.joyofbaking.com/flour.html.

Folger, Tim. "Does the Universe Exist If We're Not Looking?" *Discover* Magazine, last modified 2002, accessed 2011, http://discovermagazine.com/2002/jun/featuniverse/?searchterm=Tim%20Folger.

Green, Denzil. "Measuring Spoons." practicallyedible.com, last modified 2010, accessed 2010, http://www.practicallyedible.com/edible.nsf/pages/measuringspoons.

Gregory, Jennifer. "The History of Popcorn Poppers." *American Chronicle*, accessed 2010, http://www.americanchronicle.com/articles/view/141289.

"Griswold Cast Iron." *Black Iron* (blog), last modified 2009, accessed 2011, http://blackirondude.blogspot.com/2009/04/griswold-cast-iron.html.

"Guide to Griswold Iron Kitchen Item Collecting." essortment.com, accessed 2011, http://www.essortment.com/guide-griswold-iron-kitchen-item-collecting-66403.html.

"History and Benefit of Juicers." Best Juicer Reviews, accessed 2011, http://www.best-juicer-reviews.com/juicers.html.

"History and Legends of Popcorn, Cracker Jack & Popcorn Balls." What's Cooking America, accessed 2010, http://whatscookingamerica.net/History/PopcornHistory.htm.

"History of Coffee." National Coffee Association of U.S.A., Inc, accessed 2011, http://www.ncausa.org/i4a/pages/index.cfm?pageid=68.

"History of Cookbooks." essortment, accessed 2011, http://www.essortment.com/historical-information.

"History of Cookbooks." HubPages, accessed 2011, http://www.hubpages.com/hub/history-of-cookbooks.

"History of Ironing." Old and Interesting, accessed 2011, http://www.oldandinteresting.com/antique-irons-smoothers-mangles.aspx.

"History of Matches." Swedish Match.com, accessed 2011, http://www.swedishmatch.com/en/Our-business/Lights/History-of-matches.

"History of Orange Juice." The Best of Raw Food, accessed 2011, www.thebestofrawfood.com.

"History of Pies." What's Cooking America, accessed 2010, whatscookingamerica.net/History/PieHistory.htm.

"History of Popcorn." Popcorn, accessed 2010, http://www.popcorn.org/EncyclopediaPopcornica/WelcometoPopcornica/HistoryofPopcorn/tabid/106/Default.aspx.

"History of Popcorn Poppers." Popcorn, accessed 2010, http://www.popcorn.org/EncyclopediaPopcornica/WelcometoPopcornica/HistoryofPopcorn/tabid/106/Default.aspx.

"History of Tea." essortment.com, accessed 2011, http:// www.essortment.com/history-tea-40678.html.

"Home Pressure Canning Foods." PickYourOwn.org, accessed 2011, http://www.pickyourown.org/pressure_canning_directions.htm.

"How to Use a Wood Stove Damper." ehow.com, http://www.ehow.com/how_4829435_use-wood-stove-damper.html.

James, Dennis. "Schrodinger's Cat vs Occam's Razor." quantumpork.com, last modified 2008, accessed 2011, http://www.quantumpork.com/index.php?option=com_content&view=article&id=27:schrodinger-cat&catid=30:qp-cosmology&Itemid=13.

"Japanese Kitchen Knife Types and Styles." Zknives, accessed 2011, http://www.zknives.com.

"JUICE-KING J.K.-30 Manual Fruit Juicer." Worth Point, last modified 2008, accessed 2011, http://www.worthpoint.com/worthopedia/used-vintage-juice-king-j-k-30-manual-fruit.

Kirshenblatt-Gimblett, Barbara. "Kitchen Judaism." Getting Comfortable in New York: The Jewish Home Beautiful, accessed 2011, http://www.nyu.edu/classes/bkg/web/kitchenjudaism.pdf.

"Kitchen Dictionary: nutmeg." Food.com, accessed 2010, http://www.food.com/library/nutmeg-333.

"Knife Types." Kitchen Emporium, accessed 2011, http://www.kitchenemporium.com.

"Knife Types and Shapes." Knife Merchant, accessed 2011, http:// www.knifemerchant.com.

Ladymermaid. "Tips for Collecting Griswold Cast Iron Cookware." helium.com, accessed 2011, http://www.helium.com/items/1445154-tips-for-collecting-griswold-cast-iron-cookware.

Lahey, Anita. "The Better Clothespin." *American Heritage: Invention & Technology* Magazine, accessed 2011, http://www.americanheritage.com/.invention&technologymagazine.

Lamar, Cyriaque. "7 Common Foods That Can Actually Get You High." Cracked.com, last modified 2008, accessed 2010, http://www.cracked.com/article_16178_7-common-foods-that-can-actually-get-you-high.html.

"Learn More About Match History." Arenco.com, accessed 2011 http://arenco.com/website1/1.0.1.0/101/1/.

Lepore, Jill. "Our Own Devices." *The New Yorker,* last modified 2008, accessed 2011, http://www.newyorker.com/arts/critics/books/2008/05/12/080512crbo_books_lepore.

Lifshey, Earl. "The Saga of Landers, Frary & Clark." The Toaster Museum Foundation, accessed 2011, http:// www.toaster.org/landers.html.

Lindamood, Katy. "How to Use a Measuring Spoon." ehow.com, accessed 2011, http://www.ehow.com/print/how_2304568_use-measuring-spoon.html.

"Lovell Wringer and Washer." Beatty Museum & Historical Society in Beatty, Nevada, last modified 2010, accessed 2011, http:// beattymuseum.org/lovell_wringer.html.

"Maple Syrup." Encylopedia: Food Terms, accessed 2010, http://www.foodterms.com/encyclopedia/maple-syrup/index.html.

Mayer, Laura. "Pie." *Time*, last modified 2008, accessed 2010, http://www.time.com/time/printout/0,8816,1862315,00.html.

Maxwell, Lee M., Ph D. "Wringers, Wringer Benches and Mangles." Save Womens Lives: History of Washing Machines. Eaton, accessed 2003, books.google.com.

"Measuring Spoon History." Timeline-Goggle Search, accessed 2011, http:// twurl.nl/o0rvfx.

Mielziner, Charlotte. "The proper use and care of a butcher knife." Helium: Cookware & Cutlery, last modified August 22, 2009, accessed 2011, http://www.helium.com/items/1562446-proper-use-and-care-of-a-butcher-knife.

Mintz, Stephen. "Food In America." *Digital History*, last modified 2010, accessed 2011, http://www.digital-history.uh.edu/historyonline/food.cfm.

"More Home Canning Tips." PickYourOwn.org, accessed 2011, http://www.pickyourown.org/canningtips.php.

Moyer, Sandy. "Successful Home Canning." BellaOnline.com, accessed 2011, http://bellaonline.com/articles/art2816.asp.

Myers, Susanne. "The History of Pie." EzineArticles, accessed 2010, http://ezinearticles.com/?The-History-of-Pie&id=962195.

"Nutmeg." The Vaults of Erowid, accessed 2010, http://erowid.org/plants/nutmeg/nutmeg.shtml.

"Nutmeg: from The Encyclopedia of Psychoative Substances by Richard Ruydgley, Little, Brown and Company (1998)." moodfood.com, accessed 2010, http://moodfoods.com/nutmeg/index.html.

"On Making Pastry." chestofbooks.com, accessed 2010, http://www.chestofbooks.com/food/recipes/Young-Housekeeper/On-Making-Pastry.html.

"Pastry." The Free Online Dictionary, Thesaurus and Encyclopedia, accessed 2010, http://www.thefreedictionary.com/pastry.

"Pasta Shapes." National Pasta Association, accessed 2011, http://www.ilovepasta.org/shapes.htm.

"Pastry 101." baking911.com, accessed 2010, http://www.baking911.com/pastry/101_intro.htm.

Penny, Dave. "Little Miss Cornshucks." Black Cat Rockabilly Europe, accessed 2010, http://www.rockabillyeurope.com/references/messages/little_miss_cornshucks.htm.

"Potato and Vegetable Mashers." Feeding America: The Historic American Cookbook Project, accessed 2010, http://digital.lib.msu.edu/projects/cookbooks/html/object_075.html.

"Practical Household Devices." Periodicals, Home Economics: Good housekeeping: April 1911, Volume 53, Number 2. Mann Library, Cornell University, Ithaca, NY. http://hearth.library.cornell.edu/cgi/t/text/text-idx?c=hearth;idno=6417403_1339_002.

"Priscilla – Trademark by Leyse Aluminum Company." Trademarkia, accessed 2011, http://www.trademarkia.com.

Rock, James M and Peckham, Brian Winter. "Recession, depression, and war: The Wisconsin aluminum cookware industry, 1920-1941." Wisconsin Magazine of History Archives. 1996-2006, accessed 2011, http://www.wisconsinhistory.org/wmh/archives.

"Safety Match History." Timeline – Google Search, accessed 2011, http://twurl.nl/b0xk8m.

"Schrodinger's Cat." Whatis.com, accessed 2011, http://whatis.techtarget.com/definition/0,,sid9_gci341236,00.html.

"Sifting Flour." KitchenSavvy, last modified 2005, accessed 2010, http://www.kitchensavvy.com/journal/2005/07/sifting_flour.html.

"Soap and Detergent Industry." Gale Encyclopedia of US History, last modified 2006, accessed 2011, http://www.answers.com/topic/soap-and-detergent-industry.

"Soap Saver." Feeding America: The Historic American Cookbook Project, accessed 2011, http://digital.lib.msu.edu/projects/cookbooks/html/ object_088.html.

"Tea's Wonderful History." Chinese Historical and Cultural Project, accessed 2011, http://www.chcp.org/tea.html.

"The Art of Chinese Tea." Ten Ren Tea, accessed 2011, http://www.tenren.com/teahistory.html.

"The Different Types of Knives That Are Used as Tools." ArticlesBase.Com, accessed 2011, http://www.articlesbase.com.

"The Griswold Story." Santa Fe Trading Post, accessed 2011, http://santafetradingpost.com/griswold_history.html.

"The History of Coffee." A Brief History of Coffee and Coffee Timeline, accessed 2011, http://www.2basnob.com/coffee-history.html.

"The History of Popcorn Poppers." Article Dashboard, accessed 2010, http://www.articledashboard.com/Article/The-History-of-Popcorn-Poppers/785564.

"The History of Soap Making." Black Pearl Botanicals, accessed 2011, http://www.blackpearlbotanicals.com/soap_history.htm.

"The History of Soap Making." Signature Soapworks, accessed 2011, http://www.signaturesoapworks.com/history.html.

"The History of Soap Making." Soap Making Fun, accessed 2011, http://www.soapmakingfun.com/making-homemade-soap/history-of-soap-making.shtml.

"The Museum Gallery of Objects." Feeding America: The Historic American Cookbook Project, last modified 2005, accessed 2011, http://www.digital.lib.msu.edu/projects/cookbooks/.

"The Soap." Marseille Provence, accessed 2011, http://www.marseille-tourisme.com/en/in-marseille/what-to-do/tradition/the-soap/.

"Types of Knives." Knife Depot, accessed 2011, http://www.knife-depot.com.

"Types of Kitchen Knives and Their Specific Uses." KitchenKnivesCookware.Com, accessed 2011, http://www.kitchenknivescookware.com.

"Uncertainty Principle." Knierim, Thomas, ed. TheBigView.Com, accessed 2011, http://www.thebigview.com.

"Understanding Bacon." ehow.com, accessed 2011, http://www.ehow.com/facts_5192050_bacon-nutrition-information.html.

"Weights and Measures – History." City of Brockton, accessed 2011, http://www.brockton.ma.us/Departments/sealer_history.aspx.

"What are Mason Jars?" wiseGEEK.com, accessed 2011, http://wisegeek.com/what-are-mason-jars.htm.

"What are the different Griswold TMs?" Griswold and Cast Iron Information, accessed 2011, http://www.griswoldandwagner.com/faq.html.

"What is a Mangle?" wiseGEEK.com, accessed 2011, http://wisegeek.com/what-is-a-mangle.htm.

"What is the History of Popcorn?" essortment.com, accessed 2010, http://www.essortment.com/history-popcorn-41743.html.

Wiggins, Pamela. "Collecting Heavy Metal – Griswold Cast Iron." About.com Antiques, http://<antiques.about.com/cs/miscellaneous/a/aa013000.htm.

"Wonder Shredder Recipes." *Favorite Tested Recipes: Featuring the Wonder Shredder and Grater.* 250,000 Edition. Dixon Prosser, Inc., New York.

Supplemental Illustration Credits

Page 6—"Wonder Shredder Recipes." *Favorite Tested Recipes: Featuring the Wonder Shredder and Grater.* 250,000 Edition. Dixon Prosser, Inc., New York. Private Collection.

Page 128—"Ice Cream Mold, Patent No. 576.395 (Feb. 2, 1897). Alfred L. Cralle." Notable Pittsburgh Inventors, Carnegie Library. http://www.carnegielibrary.org/research/pittsburgh/patentees/cralle.html.

Page 196—"Thomas Jefferson Maccaroni Machine." Library of Congress. http://memory.loc.gov/mss/mcc/027/0001.jpg

Page 198—"Varieties of Pasta" *Pasta*. http://en.wikipedia.org/wiki/Pasta

Page 212—"Columbia Scale." Practical Household Devices. Periodicals, Home Economics: Good housekeeping: April 1911, Volume 53, Number 2. Mann Library, Cornell University, Ithaca, NY. http://hearth.library.cornell.edu/cgi/t/text/text-idx?c=hearth;idno=6417403_1339_002

Page 218—"Anchor Brand Wringers. Postcard: H. D. Thompson & Co., Malone, NY. Private Collection.

INDEX

RECIPE INDEX

ABOUT THE AUTHOR

Richard Snodgrass

Richard Snodgrass has been artist in residence at the Helene Wurlitzer Foundation in Taos, New Mexico, and at LightWork, University of Syracuse. He is also the recipient of a fellowship from the Pennsylvania Council on the Arts. His photographs are included in the permanent collection of the Oakland Museum of Art and in private collections and galleries nationwide. His books include the critically acclaimed novel *There's Something in the Back Yard* and the photographic commemoration of the Flight 93 Temporary Memorial, *An Uncommon Field*. Selections of *Kitchen Things* originally appeared in *TABLE* Magazine, where he is a regular contributor. He lives in Pittsburgh, Pennsylvania, with his wife, Marty, and two indomitable female tuxedo cats, raised from feral kittens, named Frankie and Becca.

For more information, go to www.rsnodgrass.com.

JOIN THE *KITCHEN THINGS* COMMUNITY ON FACEBOOK!

Post photographs of your own kitchen things, tell your own kitchen things stories, and share farm-kitchen recipes.
www.facebook.com/kitchen.things.richard.snodgrass